HALF TRUTHS

Half Truths:
God Helps Those Who Help Themselves and Other Things the Bible Doesn't Say

Half Truths
978-1-7910-2847-3
978-1-5018-1388-7 *eBook*
978-1-5018-1389-4 *Large Print*

Half Truths:
Youth Study Book
978-1-5018-1398-6
978-1-5018-1399-3 *eBook*

Half Truths: DVD
978-1-5018-1392-4

Half Truths:
Youth Leader Guide
978-1-5018-1400-6
978-1-5018-1401-3 *eBook*

Half Truths: Leader Guide
978-1-5018-1390-0
978-1-5018-1391-7 *eBook*

For more information, visit www.AdamHamilton.com.

Also by Adam Hamilton

24 Hours That Changed the World

Christianity and World Religions

Christianity's Family Tree

Confronting the Controversies

Enough

Final Words from the Cross

Forgiveness

John

Leading Beyond the Walls

Love to Stay

Making Sense of the Bible

Not a Silent Night

Revival

Seeing Gray in a World of Black and White

Selling Swimsuits in the Arctic

Speaking Well

The Call

The Journey

The Way

Unleashing the Word

When Christians Get It Wrong

Why?

ADAM HAMILTON

Author of *24 Hours That Changed the World*, *The Journey*, and *The Way*

HALF TRUTHS

GOD HELPS THOSE WHO HELP THEMSELVES AND OTHER THINGS THE BIBLE DOESN'T SAY

Abingdon Press / Nashville

HALF TRUTHS:
GOD HELPS THOSE WHO HELP THEMSELVES
AND OTHER THINGS THE BIBLE DOESN'T SAY

ISBN 978-1-7910-2847-3

First hardcover edition 978-1-5018-1387-0 is cataloged under Library of Congress Control Number 2016001837.

MANUFACTURED IN THE UNITED STATES OF AMERICA

Dedicated to the memory of
Harry Emerson Fosdick and Leslie Weatherhead,
two of my heroes among pastors for the way they invited their
parishioners and readers to engage their intellects as well as
their hearts and not to settle for a religion of half truths

CONTENTS

INTRODUCTION

Most of us as Christians have things we believe, and tell others, and even count on, that we've not carefully examined. Some of the things we accept and repeat to others sound so true, and we've believed them for so long, that they become what some call "sacred cows"—things above question or criticism. When these beliefs are questioned we become defensive or irritated. We may even worry that if the beliefs aren't true, the rest of our faith may crumble.

I don't think this book will make your faith crumble. But to the degree that I'm questioning something you've held deeply and repeated often, it might unnerve or irritate you. It's okay to say: I think the author gets it wrong in this chapter. Maybe I did. Go on to the next chapter and see what you think. Hopefully I got it right in at least one of the chapters. And remember, I'm not suggesting that these statements are entirely untrue, merely that they are half true. (Okay, some may be less than half true, but certainly there is some truth in each of them.)

Here's why it's important to examine these particular half truths: I think they can sometimes hurt people. I think they can lead people to conclusions about God that not only are untrue but that may push some people away from God. Some of these half truths are used to avoid careful thinking about complex issues. Some are used to justify our own biases or prejudices. Some, when spoken to others, can bring pain.

All of us occasionally use half truths. In fact, the subtitle of this book may be a half truth! My publisher and I discussed several subtitles and finally settled on this one: *God Helps Those Who Help Themselves and Other Things the Bible Doesn't Say*. But the truth is that you *can* find Bible passages to support nearly every one of the half truths we'll discuss. For that matter, you can find Bible passages to support all kinds of things. People who beat their children can support their practice from Scripture: "Those who withhold the rod hate their children" (Proverbs 13:24). I was taught as a teen that Christians were not to drink wine, for "Wine is a mocker; beer a carouser" (Proverbs 20:1). When a young woman is repeatedly abused by her husband, her parents can urge her to stay with him because "I hate divorce, says the LORD" (Malachi 2:16 NRSV).

Scriptures must be interpreted. Sometimes their meanings seem to conflict, or a particular message given in one context appears to be contradicted in another context. It is important to read any Scripture in the light of its context and the Bible's broader message and themes. It is not enough to find a passage or two or six to support a particular view. We interpret all Scripture in the light of Jesus' life and teachings, as well as with the help of the Spirit's witness, the wisdom of scholars, and our intellect and life experience.

Because Scriptures must be interpreted, you and I may sometimes disagree about our interpretations and other issues of faith. This was brought home to me recently when I spoke at a conference on one of the topics in this book, "Everything Happens for a Reason." I was approached by a lifelong Christian, a man who for years had served on the staff of his church. He said, "Your talk tonight really unnerved me at first.

I've always believed that everything happens for a reason. I always tell people this to comfort them when things go wrong." I was expecting him to say, "But now that I've heard your talk on this, I understand that this may not be entirely true. I'm going to be more careful in what I say to people enduring suffering." Of course, that's not what he told me. He said, "Well, I don't know about all that stuff you talked about tonight. But I do know one thing: everything happens for a reason." So much for the compelling case I had presented!

I'll end this short introduction with another experience I had this week as I was ministering with an individual. Her little sister, a teenager, had just died tragically. I stopped by to offer comfort and care. Through her tears the young woman told me, "I know it was her time, but I don't understand why God would take my little sister now. She was just a kid." The young woman had grown up learning that whatever happened, it must be the will of God. God must have predetermined that it was her sister's time to die. Though I may have disagreed, it would not have been helpful to question her assumptions at that moment. I simply hugged her, prayed for her, and offered to talk further in the days ahead. But my hope in writing this book is to invite you to question assumptions such as the young woman's before you find yourself in a situation like hers, when those assumptions might raise questions that challenge your faith.

Yes, there is some truth to be found in the "truths" we'll explore in the pages that follow. I invite you, though, to consider whether these truths are as Christian or as true as you may suppose. And, if I'm right, I hope you might think twice before you say them again.

More than that, I hope that examining these and other half truths will lead you to the greater truths we find in Jesus Christ.

1.

EVERYTHING HAPPENS
FOR A REASON

[Then Moses said to the Israelites,] I call heaven and earth to witness against you today that I have set before you life and death, blessings and curses. Choose life so that you and your descendants may live, loving the LORD your God, obeying him, and holding fast to him; for that means life to you and length of days.

—Deuteronomy 30:19-20a NRSV

1.

EVERYTHING HAPPENS FOR A REASON

Has anyone ever said to you, "Everything happens for a reason"? Most of us have heard that statement from someone at some point. Many of us have said it to someone else.

The statement is true if, in saying it, we mean that we live in a world of cause and effect. Actions create consequences. Our own choices produce results. A result of choosing to text while driving may be a collision in which someone is injured. In the Scripture at the beginning of this chapter, Moses is preaching to the Israelites about cause and effect. Choosing to live under God's law of love for God and neighbor leads to life and peace for the community.

Usually, however, when we say "Everything happens for a reason" we're not talking about cause and effect. Most often, we're speaking in response to suffering. When something bad has happened and we're trying to help someone through a difficult time, we say "It was meant to be." When someone dies unexpectedly, we hear "It must have been their time" or "It was part of the plan" or "It must have been God's will." We seek to console—and others seek to console us—by saying that God has a particular purpose for bringing about (or at least allowing) situations in which people suffer. We may assume that while we don't yet understand why it had to happen, all events in our lives unfold according to God's predetermined and immutable plan. Since God is in charge of everything, whatever happens—a personal setback, an untimely death, a natural disaster—reflects the will and purposes of God.

If we extend this logic, we can arrive at some extremes that seem silly:

- "God meant for my team to win (or lose) the World Series."
- "Honey, I'm sorry I forgot your birthday. It must have been the will of God."

And we can get to some very troubling questions:

- "Why would God will millions of Jews to die in the Holocaust?"
- "Does God really want little children to die in a school shooting?"

So, does everything happen for a reason? At best, this is a half truth. I'd love to scrub it from the list of things we say to comfort people when they are going through difficult situations. The notion that God picks winners and losers in professional sports or the stock market, let alone that God intends car accidents, criminal acts, genocide, or mass murder, surely is worth examining.*

The Problem of Personal Responsibility

If we examine the notion that everything happens for a reason, the first problem is that it eliminates the concept of personal responsibility for our actions. If everything happens according to God's immutable plan, then whatever I do must have been God's will.

---

* Much of what I've written in this chapter I've covered in more detail in my book, *Why? Making Sense of God's Will* (Abingdon Press, 2011). In that book I also address the questions of intercessory prayer and the specificity of God's will for our lives.

God isn't going to change it. In fact, God must have needed and wanted me to do it; otherwise, God would not have let it happen.

If I cheat on my wife, it must have been part of God's plan. If my wife and children suffer because of my cheating, that must have been God's will for them, even if they can't fathom why God ordained it to happen. If I drink and drive and someone is killed as a result, it must have been the victim's "time." Yes, I did a terrible thing, but the devil didn't make me do it. Instead, God used me to accomplish some greater purpose. I cannot be held responsible for my actions; I was only doing what God willed me to do.

The Problem of God's Responsibility

A second problem with the notion that everything happens for a reason is that it makes God responsible for everyone's actions. If God actually intended for everything to happen, then God is responsible for every terrible thing that happens in our world. It would mean that tragedies do not happen in spite of God's will but because of it.

Consider how this idea plays out by taking as examples some news stories I saw the week before I prepared a sermon on this topic.

- A two-year-old unzipped his mother's purse in a Walmart, pulled out a handgun, thought it was a toy, pointed it at his mother, and pulled the trigger. It must have been God's plan for her to die and for the toddler to grow up and go through life carrying the emotional burden of having killed his mother.

- Air Asia Flight 8501 crashed in bad weather, leaving 162 people dead. It must have been each of the passengers' "time." God caused the disaster, and the deaths of everyone on board were a part of God's plan. The grieving of loved ones left behind, too, was meant to fulfill some part of God's plan. There was no point in searching for the airplane's black box. There was nothing to learn from the flight data recorders, because the crash was orchestrated by God. Any improvements in airline safety that might have resulted from learning and applying lessons from this crash would have been pointless, because the next crash would also be God's will, no matter what safeguards human beings might design.

If this way of thinking is true, then every rape, every murder, every act of child abuse, every war, every terrible storm or earthquake that claims people's lives, every child that dies of starvation—all these are part of God's plan. That is the awful truth we must confront when we buy into the half truth that everything happens for a divinely ordained reason.

The Problem of Fatalism and Indifference

A third problem with the notion that everything happens for a reason, and that whatever happens is part of God's plan, is that it leads to fatalism and indifference. A fatalist thinks, "Whatever is going to happen, will happen. Whatever will be, will be. We are powerless to change it."

If you're a committed fatalist, there is no reason ever to wear a seat belt; if you are meant to die in a car accident, you will. If you are not meant to die, you won't. If you take a fatalistic view, why work out, eat healthy foods, or take care of your body? After all, when it's your time, it's your time. It won't matter how much you exercise, or whether you eat bacon three times a day. Diagnosed with cancer? If you're a fatalist, don't waste time seeing an oncologist. To seek treatment would be to resist God's will; it was God, after all, who gave you the cancer in the first place. In fact, the entire medical profession, far from being God's instruments of healing, would seem to be working against God's plans. (Perhaps it is worth noting here the relationship between the words *fatal* and *fatalism*.)

Consider how this way of thinking plays out when it comes to politics. Many who believe that whatever happens must have been the will of God suddenly lose this perspective when it comes to politics. Republicans struggle to believe a Democratic president's election was "the will of God." Democrats, likewise, struggle with the idea that a Republican president was God's choice for the office. Do we really believe that everything that happens is God's will?

Or think of sports. Does God really "fix" the outcome of the Super Bowl, the World Series, and the Olympics?

Is this really how things work? Is God calling us to be fatalists?

God's Providence and Sovereignty

Theologians speak of God's purposes and way of working in the world as the doctrine of divine providence. *Providence* is a noun that is closely related to the verb *provide*. The term typically refers to God's governance of the cosmos, including our world and everything in it. Christians believe that God superintends the universe and oversees what happens on our planet.

Closely linked to providence is another attribute of God: divine sovereignty. The word *sovereignty* typically expresses the idea of authority or rule. In any given place, a sovereign is the highest authority. A sovereign depends on no one else for the power to rule. Christians affirm that God's authority encompasses all creation. As our Jewish brothers and sisters say regularly in their prayers, God is "King of the universe." Because God is the ultimate authority, all power and honor, glory and dominion ultimately belong to God.

Though Christians share a belief in God's providence and sovereignty, they often interpret these concepts in very different ways.

Though Christians share a belief in God's providence and sovereignty, they often interpret these concepts in very different ways. Some tend toward a view of God as micromanager, involved intimately each day in every detail of the world's operation. Others believe that God follows a hands-off approach, like an absentee landlord who created everything and then stepped away to let the world run itself. Still others believe the truth is somewhere between the two positions. As a result of these varying interpretations, it's worth taking some time here to look at the contrasting views of how God's rule is carried out.

Calvinism and Theological Determinism

John Calvin (1509–1564) was a brilliant lawyer, theologian, and pastor. He was one of the most important figures in the Protestant Reformation. At age twenty-seven he wrote his book *Institutes of the Christian Religion*, which not only was an influential book in his day, but shaped much of Protestant thinking long after his lifetime. Writing in opposition to Catholicism, he outlined Protestant theology as he conceived it.

One of the defining emphases of Calvin's theology involved his understanding of God's sovereignty. Calvin seemed to believe that for God to be sovereign—that is, to be the highest authority and to have dominion over the universe—then God must will and, in some ultimate sense, *cause* everything that happens. If something happens that is not God's will, Calvin argued, then God does not in fact have dominion over everything. This view is sometimes referred to as theological determinism.

Absolutely everything, Calvin believed, happens by God's will and command. Had science in Calvin's time known about human cells and atoms, he would have said that God was directing creation down to the smallest particles. As Calvin wrote in the *Institutes*, "No wind ever rises or rages without [God's] special command."[1] Every aspect of the daily weather, from thunderstorms to gentle rain and from gales to soft breezes, is decreed by a God who manages everything to the nth degree.

It was natural for Calvin to profess that whatever happens in people's lives reflects God's desire and purpose, and in fact there is some scriptural basis for this view. In a time before humans understood weather patterns, people believed that God withheld the rain or gave it. So, for example, we read in Scripture about the punishing drought in Israel during Elijah's time. To someone like Elijah, the weather was not about atmospheric conditions but about God's reaction to the behavior of human beings.

I'm not denying the fact that God could cause the rain or bring storms. In the case of Elijah's drought, this was a direct act of God. Yet this particular episode in Scripture is not meant to teach us about how the weather works, but rather, God's particular judgment on the sins of the Israelites in the ninth century before Christ. Today I believe we're right to question whether the rain, snow, and sunshine are really God's doing, or the result of the complex forces guiding our weather patterns. Our forecasters are not prophets testifying to God's plans for the weather; instead, they examine satellite images and monitor weather patterns to tell us—most of the time, with a decent degree of accuracy—what our weather will be like tomorrow, the next day, and the next.

Consider another example. Calvin believed that a woman's ability to conceive a child was the result of God's will. This clearly was the view of infertility held by many in Scripture. They frequently noted that God "closed up" or "opened" a woman's womb. Just as Calvin and the Old Testament writers didn't understand the natural forces causing the weather, they didn't understand human fertility or the unseen physiological and biochemical factors that affect pregnancy. Yet for Calvin, even if he had understood these factors they may have made no difference to him. He believed that God's sovereignty requires that everything, including the minute details of physiology and biochemistry, is under God's daily direction.

According to this view, even our thoughts and feelings are governed by God. You might think you've had an original idea, but in Calvin's reality God placed that idea in your mind. You didn't decide to take that job offer or even take out the garbage; God, guiding your thoughts, decided those things for you. Thus for Calvin, everything that happens, for good or bad, is "fixed by [God's] decree."[2]

One corollary to this view, and the one for which Calvin is especially known, is a particular focus of theological determinism called predestination. Predestination means that God has predetermined everything that happens—that life unfolds according to a script God has written before any of us are born. But one of the implications of this belief is that God has predetermined, before we are born, whether we will accept his salvation or be among the damned.

According to this view, we have no choice about whether or not we will accept the grace of God. Before you were born, you were predestined to be either among the elect or, by not being chosen for election, among the damned. If you are among the elect, God's grace is irresistible to you. No matter how hard you might try to reject Christ, you will be saved. If you are not one of the elect, hell is your certain fate, regardless of how you live your life or how much you desire salvation.

Many Christians struggle with the idea of predestination. The view seems capricious and unjust to many of us. John Wesley, the founder of Methodism, taught that God wills all humanity to be saved. Through what Wesley called prevenient grace, God works in human beings to make it possible for us to respond to

God's love and mercy. Some choose to accept God's saving grace while others reject it, but at least this salvation was offered by God to all, and it was God's will that all would receive it.

Through what Wesley called prevenient grace, God works in human beings to make it possible for us to respond to God's love and mercy.

Theological determinism—the idea that all things happen according to God's plan and will and that God is directing everything—is very appealing to some. In a world where there is much uncertainty, where doubt and questioning are such a prominent part of life, one reaction is a retreat toward absolute certainty. And in a world that seems so out of control, some find it comforting to imagine every detail of life being controlled by the plan and will of God.

As noted, Calvin could claim some scriptural support for his position, and a number of biblical authors clearly saw God's sovereignty in these terms. Often cited in this connection is Matthew 10:29 where Jesus states, "Aren't two sparrows sold for a small coin? But not one of them will fall to the ground without your Father knowing about it already." But God's knowledge of something is different from God's command that this or that event happen. The overarching message of the Bible does not seem to make God a micromanager directing everything according to his will. Instead, God is more like a parent who invites his children to make their own choices, even knowing they will sometimes make the wrong ones. We see this picture of God from the opening story of the Bible.

God Gives Humanity Dominion

In the story of Adam and Eve, God tells them, "Be fertile and multiply; fill the earth and master it. Take charge of the fish of the sea, the birds in the sky, and everything crawling on the ground" (Genesis 1:28). God creates the cosmos, sets the laws in motion by which the universe operates, and then gives humanity dominion, or authority. In other words, God puts people in charge of what happens on earth. Does this mean that God is not still ultimately in charge? Of course not! God remains sovereign but has given us the responsibility to rule over this planet on his behalf.

We see this same theme in the story of the garden of Eden. God places a tree in the midst of the garden and yet forbids the humans to eat from it. Have you ever wondered why God put the tree there to begin with? My own view is that this story is archetypal, and it is meant to teach us that part of being human is having to make choices between doing good and following God's path or turning away from it.

In the Bible, the very word *sin* means to miss the mark or turn from the right path. The tree illustrates the idea that being human means having the freedom to choose either the right path—God's way—or the wrong path. God doesn't determine which choice we will make. Much of the biblical story is about human beings misusing their freedom and turning away from God, and about God's work to clean up the mess.

God has given us freedom to make choices, for better or worse. So when we do something wrong, we can't blame God. We can't excuse a poor choice by saying it was always part of God's master plan. As the Creation story tells us, we are the ones who exercise dominion on God's behalf.

God has given us freedom to make choices, for better or worse. So when we do something wrong, we can't blame God.

Jesus told a parable that illustrates this point. The story involves tenants who lease a vineyard and operate it in a careless way. When the owner sends his servants to remind the wicked tenants of the owner's sovereignty and ask them to stop abusing the owner's interests, the tenants respond violently. It's clear what Jesus was talking about: human beings are the tenants farming God's earth. We are tending God's creation. God is the owner; the earth belongs to him. We are free as stewards to make choices, and we are responsible for those choices.

The idea of choice is so very important to our theology. Throughout Scripture, God shows human beings the right path and warns against pursuing the wrong path. The passage from Deuteronomy that begins this chapter is an excellent illustration. Through his servant, Moses, God has led the children of Israel out of slavery in Egypt. As they prepare to enter the

Promised Land, Moses, now an old man nearing death, has just recited the Ten Commandments and the rest of the Law. It's not the first time the Israelites have heard these commandments. But in his sermon to them, Moses reminds them one more time of what God expects of his people.

Then notice what Moses says next. He implores the Israelites,

> I call heaven and earth as my witnesses against you right now: I have set life and death, blessing and curse before you. Now choose life—so that you and your descendants will live—by loving the LORD your God, by obeying his voice, and by clinging to him. That's how you will survive and live long on the fertile land.
>
> (Deuteronomy 30:19-20a)

Speaking on God's behalf, Moses is showing the Israelites two paths into the Promised Land. One path leads to life; the other leads to death. One path involves a choice to obey and love God, which also means loving the neighbors made in God's image and seeking to do God's will in the world; the other path involves a choice to live for ourselves, without regard for God or anybody else.

Think about how this message relates to God's sovereignty and human freedom. If people are simply bound to do whatever God puts on their heart to do, what is the point of Moses' powerful and compelling challenge? The Israelites face a very real choice. They can obey God, hold fast to God, love God, and find life; or they can turn away and find death. Why call them to choose if, in reality, they have no choice in the matter?

We have been given the gift of dominion. Sometimes we use that dominion to make moral choices. Sometimes we make immoral choices that hurt ourselves or other people or that bring shame to us. And sometimes we make amoral choices. Deciding where to go to lunch today is usually not a moral decision; it's simply a choice.

Even amoral decisions, however, may involve consequences. During the summertime, my wife and I like to ride motorcycles. When the weather is warm and sunny, LaVon and I go out on our bikes. She likes to ride back roads about thirty-five miles per hour. When I'm on my own I prefer to ride on the highway. I like to ride fast. There's something exhilarating about going seventy miles per hour with the wind in your face and the concrete six inches beneath your feet. But I know that every time I get on my motorcycle, it may be the last time. I understand that I am taking a risk. My donor card on the back of my driver's license is signed. If I'm hurt or killed, is that God's will? Or was it a decision I made?

I also like to ski, and I like to get downhill fast. When I go to Colorado and pick up my skis, a big sign warns me that I agree to hold the owners of the property harmless in case of an accident on the slopes. I acknowledge that I'm about to engage in an activity with inherent risk. If I make a mistake and lose control and end up hurt, that's not the fault of the ski resort. It's not the fault of the outfitter who rented me the equipment. In the same way that I agree to hold the ski resort harmless, I cannot blame God for my choices.

Few activities are completely without risk. The only way to truly minimize risk is to lock yourself in your room and have someone serve you sanitized food under the door every day. But I don't want to live that way, and I imagine you don't either. Part of the joy of living includes the risks that come with it. Shall I blame God for the consequences of my actions?

Should I say they were the will of God or happened according to God's plan?

Of course, I am not the only person with dominion. You have it too. So does the woman who doesn't think she has a drinking problem and drives while intoxicated. So does the CEO who makes decisions that enrich him personally but eventually lead to the company's bankruptcy—and the loss of jobs for thousands of people who work there. People who hurt children have dominion, as do religious extremists who teach that God condones religious violence.

God gave us a brain, a heart, a conscience, his Spirit, the Scriptures, and the ability to interpret them as guides to help us select the right path.

I do not believe that God dictates our choices, as if we are mere puppets. Instead, God gave us a brain, a heart, a conscience, his Spirit, the Scriptures, and the ability to interpret them as guides to help us select the right path.

Deism and the Hands-Off God

If humans have dominion over the earth, you might rightly ask, "Is it all up to us? Doesn't God have a hand in the affairs of this world?"

On the opposite end of the spectrum from Calvinism is a theological philosophy called Deism. It was popular in eighteenth-century America, particularly among some of our nation's founders. In its popular form, Deism held that God created all things, set the laws of nature in motion, gave humanity dominion over the earth, then stepped away and put the whole machine on autopilot. It is almost diametrically opposed to Calvinism or theological determinism.

Deism avoids the theological problem of con-demning certain people to hell before they are born. It eludes the problem that accidents and human suffering are all part of God's plan. The problem with Deism is that it makes no room for God to be at work in our world at all. If Deism is true, then God did not liberate the Israelite slaves from Egypt. God did not speak through the prophets. God did not send Jesus to show us the way or to save us from ourselves. God's Spirit does not dwell within us. For God, creation is not an ongoing act. God is not involved in any way in our lives. In a sense, Deism does solve the problem of suffering, but it negates so much of what Christianity teaches.

Christianity asserts that God *does* seek to influence us. God *does* work in us and through us. God *did* send Jesus to save and deliver us. And God does, on some occasions and for reasons we may never fully understand, intervene in the world's affairs in miraculous ways.

When I think about what it means for God to work in us and through us, I consider what routinely happens in my life. I begin each day praying, "Lord, here I am. Please use me to do what you want with me. Help me to honor you and live for you today." And then I feel that my mission is to pay attention as I go through the day, to see where God might need me. I seek to be alert to those who are sorrowful or someone who needs help or a situation in which I might make a difference. When I approach the day that way, I have found that God speaks to me, not through some audible voice but through a gentle nudge. And because sometimes I am spiritually hard of hearing, I'm never quite sure whether it's God who is nudging me or just a random thought that came into my mind. But over time I have come to trust that when I feel that nudge to do something, I should pay attention.

I recently purchased a smartwatch. One of the reasons I bought it was for the fitness features. Every hour, it vibrates on my wrist telling me to get up and walk around. It vibrates again at various times throughout the day encouraging me to exercise. The watch, of course, doesn't force me to do anything, but it nudges, reminds, or calls me to action. That's how I experience God working in my life: I feel nudges from time to time. For me, that is how God governs and superintends.

One evening not long ago, my wife, LaVon, was out of town, so I decided to go out to dinner. As I was headed toward a particular restaurant I felt a strong urge to turn around and go to a different restaurant instead. I didn't know if it was just a random thought that came into my mind or if it was the nudging of God, but I decided to turn around and go to another restaurant. When I walked into that restaurant, a woman sitting at the front table looked at me, and her jaw dropped. "Pastor Adam," she said, "I can't believe you're here. I've been going through a really tough time. Not ten minutes ago I had been praying, 'God, can you show me some kind of sign that you still remember I'm here?' And then you walked in."

Was it just coincidence? Maybe. Or was it a "God-incidence," a situation where God led me to be in the right place at the right time? I don't believe that everything happens for a reason, but sometimes there is a reason that things happen when we are attentive to God's mission. I think God uses us and works through us as we exercise our dominion in the world. When we engage ourselves in God's rule, as we are meant to, we find joy. I experienced joy when I found myself in the middle of this God-incidence at the restaurant. And somehow a person who had been praying through a difficult time felt encouraged, strengthened, and blessed. I think this is how God most often works.

God is neither the micromanager that determinism suggests nor the absentee landlord of the Deists. These ideas are both half truths. The deeper truth, I believe, lies somewhere in between.

God Is Sovereign, Gives Freedom, and Works Through People

A member of our congregation sent me a Facebook meme that said: "Everything happens for a reason, but sometimes the reason is that you're stupid and you make bad decisions." The statement might be a little harsh, but it's a bit humorous as well. It also gets at the deeper truth between determinism and Deism. It captures far more truth than saying the results of our bad decisions—harm to ourselves and others— were really God's plan all along. The reason most things happen is not because God willed them, but because of the decisions we make or the laws that govern nature and our interaction with them.

Yet God superintends. God wrote the laws of nature. God has a will and plan for humanity. God guides us by the Spirit through the Scriptures, in church, as we pray, and through other Christians. God strengthens and walks with us. We are called and empowered to be God's hands and voice in the world, but God does not force us. God has shown us what is good and what is required of us, but he also gives us freedom to walk in his path or away from it, and that choice is what makes us human.

The Apostle Paul, on the way to Rome for his trial before the emperor, writes to the Christian community there: "We know that God works all things together for good for the ones who love God, for those who are called according to his purpose" (Romans 8:28). Many Christians know that passage by heart. But let's look at what Paul doesn't say. He doesn't say that God makes everything happen for a reason, or that whatever happens was part of God's will and plan. Rather, he says that no matter what happens, however bad it may be, God will somehow bring good out of the situation for those who love him. God will force evil to accomplish good.

I don't believe God gives his children cancer. I don't believe God causes people to commit murder. I don't believe God's will is for someone to die in a car crash. But even in all these terrible occurrences, God has a way of forcing good to come from tragedy when we trust him with it. As I look back on the most painful experiences in my life, I can see how God used them to bring about something good and beautiful. In fact, the person I am today is largely the product of my most painful experiences and what God did with them through me.

As Christians, we recognize that sometimes horrible things happen. They are part of life. But we also recognize that horrible things will never have the final word. Ultimately they become part of our journey that finally reaches its end in God's eternal kingdom. That's what Jesus' resurrection shows us. Death is not the end. Love outlasts it all. God has the final word.

At our church's Leawood campus, we have a small chapel named for a retired pastor named Ray Firestone. Ray was a part of our congregation for its first fifteen years, during which he volunteered in various ways. He once shared a quotation with me, which he said he found helpful in dealing with suffering, particularly after the death of his wife in a car accident. I have found it helpful too:

> Suffering is not God's desire for us, but it occurs in the process of life. Suffering is not given to teach us something, but through it we may learn. Suffering is not given to punish us, but sometimes it is the consequence of our sin or poor judgment. Suffering does not occur because our faith is weak, but through it our faith may be strengthened. God does not depend on human suffering to achieve his purposes, but sometimes through suffering his purposes are achieved. Suffering can either destroy us, or it can add meaning to our life.

The Bible is largely the story of human beings doing what God doesn't want them to do, of tragedies that sometimes happen in life, and of God working to comfort, heal, and redeem the human race following our missteps. God does not generally cause our suffering, but he carries us through it and brings something good from it. Some will ask about God's discipline, since the Scriptures note that "The LORD disciplines those he loves" (Proverbs 3:12 NIV). Yes, but what form does that discipline take? I tend to think it most often comes in the natural consequences of our actions. At times it is in the awareness that our actions have erected a wall between God and us. Whatever discipline God brings our way will be consistent with his justice, mercy, and love. The New Testament authors taught that on the cross, Christ himself bore the punishment that our sins deserve.* As a rule I think we should be very, very careful about attributing to God the tragedies and pain that happen in our lives.

---

* I can think of a couple of exceptions in the New Testament. Paul was temporarily struck blind, but this seems to have been a way for God to gain Paul's attention. We might hope the same was true when Elymas was struck blind in Acts 13. More perplexing, however, is the story in Acts 5 of Ananias and Sapphira, who were struck dead after lying to the apostles about money. Few assert that what happened to Ananias and Sapphira is something we can expect in today's church, though if it did it might have a dramatic impact on church giving!

One day about twenty years ago, I was in a meeting at church when I received an urgent phone call from the police. They asked if I could come right away to the hospital. A three-year-old boy named Austin had been struck by a car. I left the meeting and drove as fast as I safely could to the emergency room. When I arrived, the police officer and the chaplain met me. They told me that Austin had just passed away.

I walked into the emergency room, where I found doctors and nurses, tears in their eyes, standing around the family. And then I saw Austin's parents holding their son. One of them asked me, "Pastor Adam, would you please baptize Austin? He was never baptized." So the nurses filled a stainless steel basin with water, and I took Austin in my arms and baptized him in the name of the Father and the Son and the Holy Spirit—not because he wouldn't go to heaven otherwise but because his parents needed to know that God's covenant covered him and that he was safe in God's loving arms.

In the two decades since that awful day, Austin's parents, Todd and Kathy, have continued to be an active part of our congregation. As I watched this family, who so easily could have turned away from God after the loss of their three-year-old, I saw them instead turn closer toward God and grow deeper and more committed in their faith. Several years ago I asked Kathy if she or Todd would tell me how Austin's death had affected their faith. Here is what Kathy wrote to me by way of reply:

> At the time I had had people tell me that it was Austin's "time," and I was having a hard time believing in a God who would plan to take my child at age three. I learned that tragedies weren't necessarily part of God's plan, but that God gave us free will, and that bad things sometimes happen. Understanding this helped me to turn to God instead of away from Him.... Since Austin's death, I believe that my faith has grown and continues to grow. His death changed the way I view God and my faith. I no longer have a naive, childlike faith where God protects you from all harm and makes everything OK. It's a deeper faith that has been tested through tragedy. I know that God doesn't promise me a pain-free life, but He does promise to always be there to love me, comfort me, and guide me. My faith gives me something that people without faith don't have—HOPE. I have hope for the future and the knowledge that I will see Austin again in heaven.

Between the micromanaging God who causes everything to happen and the absentee landlord God who is not involved in our lives is a picture of God who grants human beings freedom and allows them to take risks. It is a picture of God who does not cause tragedy but uses it, of God who can directly and supernaturally intervene but usually works indirectly through people. It is a picture of God who, through the power of Jesus' resurrection, gives us assurance that in the end "death has been swallowed up by a victory" (1 Corinthians 15:54).[3]

A Prayer of Surrender

In 1755 John Wesley first led the Methodists in what became known as the Covenant Prayer. In British Methodism this prayer was used in a covenant service on the first weekend of the New Year. It is a prayer of surrender. Though God does not cause suffering, in the Covenant Prayer we yield ourselves, our entire lives, to be used by God, even if the way leads to suffering. Like many Christians, I pray some variation of the Covenant Prayer each morning. I invite you to make it your prayer.

I am no longer my own, but thine.
Put me to what thou wilt, rank me with whom thou wilt.
Put me to doing, put me to suffering.
Let me be employed for thee or laid aside for thee,
*   exalted for thee or brought low for thee.*
Let me be full, let me be empty.
Let me have all things, let me have nothing.
I freely and heartily yield all things to thy pleasure and disposal.
And now, O glorious and blessed God,
*   Father, Son, and Holy Spirit,*
*   thou art mine, and I am thine.*
So be it.
And the covenant which I have made on earth,
*   let it be ratified in heaven. Amen.*

2.

GOD HELPS THOSE WHO HELP THEMSELVES

The helpless commit themselves to you; you have been the helper of the orphan.... O LORD, you will hear the desire of the meek; you will strengthen their heart, you will incline your ear to do justice for the orphan and the oppressed.

—Psalm 10:14b, 17-18a NRSV

In my distress I called upon the LORD; to my God I cried for help. From his temple he heard my voice, and my cry to him reached his ears.... He reached down from on high, he took me; he drew me out of mighty waters.
—Psalm 18:6, 16 NRSV

I lift up my eyes to the hills—from where will my help come? My help comes from the LORD, who made heaven and earth.

—Psalm 121:1-2 NRSV

2.

GOD HELPS THOSE WHO HELP THEMSELVES

I vividly recall an episode of *The Tonight Show* from some years ago. It included one of Jay Leno's trademark "Jaywalking" segments, in which he would ask questions of random people on the street. On this occasion, he asked people to name one of the Ten Commandments. It was startling to me how many people answered him by saying, "God helps those who help themselves."

That, of course, is *not* one of the Ten Commandments.

But those who gave that erroneous answer have plenty of company. A survey by the Barna Group, a

Christian polling firm, found that better than eight in ten Americans think "God helps those who help themselves" is in the Bible. In fact, more than half of the respondents were strongly convinced that this is one of the major messages of Scripture.

For the record, the Bible contains no such verse. The statement apparently originated in Greek mythology in the fifth century before Christ. Then it was echoed by various philosophers over the next two-and-a-half millennia. Most notably, in 1736 Ben Franklin popularized it in *Poor Richard's Almanac*, helping to give the statement a permanent place in American thinking.

Even though it's not in the Bible, can we find any biblical truth in this theological idea? In one sense, I think it does capture a biblical teaching. But in two other important ways, I would argue that "God helps those who help themselves" is absolutely untrue. Instead, it sends a message that is the direct opposite of the Bible's message. So it really doesn't even rise quite to the level of a half truth—more like a "one-third" truth.

In this chapter, we'll look at ways in which we might discern some spiritual truth in this statement and, more importantly, ways in which we need to rebut some spiritual fictions.

The "One-Third" Truth

"God helps those who help themselves" is only a partial truth, but of course that doesn't mean it contains no truth at all. In fact, it hints at an important truth.

When I sit down to eat, I say a mealtime blessing. But just because I prayed doesn't mean food magically appears on my plate. That would be a good way to go hungry. I worked for my supper by earning a paycheck. We went to the effort of buying groceries and preparing the meal. When I bow my head before eating, I am thanking God for the capacity to earn a living. I'm thanking God for a planet that sustains our life, for all the farmers who work to plant and harvest the crops, for the truckers who brought it to the grocery store, and for the people who handled it. Ultimately, the food I eat comes from God. But it only appears because I and many others did our part.

The same considerations apply to employment. If I were unemployed and simply sat around praying, "God please give me a job," it might be a long wait before I became employed once more. Instead, it would be important for me to prepare a résumé, actively look for job openings, submit applications, go to interviews, and try to convince employers that I was well qualified for the job. Without this work on my part, it's likely I would remain unemployed.

I think of a couple who were trying to sell their home some years ago. They prayed for a buyer. At church, they turned in prayer request cards for the home to sell. They actually borrowed a plastic statue of St. Joseph from a friend and buried it headfirst next to the real estate sign. Months went by without a nibble. All along, their real estate agent had told them they were asking too much for the property. The couple came and spoke with me about it, expressing their disappointment with God for not answering their prayers. I suggested that, given the agent's counsel, what they really had been praying for was that God would send them someone willing to pay $10,000 more than their home was worth. Finally they listened to the agent's advice and lowered the price by $10,000. The house sold within a few days.

The moral of these stories: God is not going to drop food on your table, force someone to hire you for a job when someone more qualified is available, or make people spend more for your home than it is worth. We can pray and pray, but we also have to do some work in the process. God blesses us with brains, strength, and wisdom. God provides other people (such as the couple's real estate agent) to advise us. All these are God's gifts to us, but it is up to us to use them. So we pray—*and* we work.

Paul had to address this same issue when he wrote to the new Christians in the Aegean port city of Thessalonika. On his second missionary journey Paul had started a church there, one of the first on the European continent. He had taught people to trust in Jesus Christ—and trust that Jesus might come back at any moment, and probably very soon. As a result, some of Paul's converts mistakenly came to believe that trusting in Jesus meant they could quit their jobs and wait for his imminent return. They thought they didn't have to work or be careful in their spending; God would provide for them.

When word of this reached Paul, he wrote to the little church with these instructions:

> When we were with you we were giving you this command: "If anyone doesn't want to work, they shouldn't eat." We hear that some of you are living an undisciplined life. They aren't working,

> but they are meddling in other people's business.
> By the Lord Jesus Christ, we command and
> encourage such people to work quietly and put
> their own food on the table.
>
> (2 Thessalonians 3:10-12)

Benedictine monks use a Latin phrase *ora et labora*. It means "Pray and work." That was Paul's message to the Thessalonians. He did not teach that trusting in Jesus means you pray and then God takes care of everything. Our faith is meant to move us to action even as we trust in God. We pray, and we work.

I was thinking about the phrase "Pray and work" on March 7, 2015. All over the country that day, people were marking the fiftieth anniversary of a civil rights march in Selma, Alabama—a day that came to be called "Bloody Sunday." You may know quite a bit of the story. In 1965, African Americans in Alabama were being blocked from exercising their right to vote. In order to register, they were subjected to absurd tests and questions no one could answer. As one example, African Americans had to guess the exact number of jellybeans in a large jar before they could register to vote. The clear intent was to keep them disenfranchised.

In response, people began to organize, and churches were at the center of it. During a peaceful demonstration, church deacon Jimmie Lee Jackson was shot by a state trooper and later died of his wounds. At a meeting at Zion Methodist Church in Marion, Alabama, a call went out for a larger, nonviolent march from Selma to Montgomery, Alabama. On Sunday, March 7, 1965, approximately six hundred marchers gathered for worship in their churches, then met at Brown Chapel African Methodist Episcopal Church. They began with prayer, and then they went about nonviolently protesting for their rights. They prayed for strength, and then they worked.

Leading the march was John Lewis, a young seminary student, who as of this writing has served in the United States Congress for almost thirty years. The other leader was Hosea Williams, an ordained Baptist pastor who went on to serve in politics and social causes. The group planned to march fifty-four miles, but they had barely gotten underway before police blocked them as they crossed the Edmund Pettus Bridge. The police attacked—some were on horseback—and the people who started their day in church were physically beaten for their efforts to march. More than fifty were hospitalized. John Lewis suffered a fractured skull. These church people did not simply pray and wait for God to fix things. They lived out the idea of *ora et labora*. They prayed and worked. They were willing to sacrifice, and even to risk death, because they believed God was calling them to work on behalf of a just and moral cause. Bloody Sunday was a turning point in the civil rights movement. It galvanized more support for the cause. Two days later, Martin Luther King, Jr. came to Selma and led another march. And then another. Later that year, Congress passed the Voting Rights Act.

As Scripture reveals over and over again, God works through people. We are the instruments God uses to change the world.

So in a sense there is truth to the idea that God helps those who help themselves. We don't sit around waiting for God to miraculously right the wrongs in society. As Scripture reveals over and over again, God works through people. We are the instruments God uses to change the world. Our times of prayer are meant to empower us for and guide us into action. Those who fought for civil rights did not simply show up at church and pray; they prayed and then marched, knowing they were likely to be beaten and arrested but that God would somehow see them through.

God's Concern for the Poor and Needy

We've seen that the saying "God helps those who help themselves" has some basis in Scripture. Now, however, I'd like to suggest two important senses in which the saying is fundamentally unbiblical.

First, this phrase is sometimes used as a way of avoiding our obligation as Christians to help others, of doing our part to love our neighbors. The fact is that some people truly cannot help themselves. And for many others who find themselves trapped in poverty or struggling financially, self-help often isn't nearly so simple as summoning the will and pulling themselves up by the bootstraps. Sometimes people are in a hole so deep that they can't climb out without help.

I remember a man I met when I was twenty-three years old. I had just graduated from seminary. The man was homeless and was asking for money. I imagined that I could help turn his life around in no time at all.

When the man saw me, he asked, "Hey, can you spare some money for lunch?"

I said, "I'll do better than that. I'll take you to lunch."

He agreed, so we went to lunch together. I happened to have a copy of our newspaper, the *Kansas City Star*. After I paid for the man's lunch, I said, "You know, I'd love to see you get a job. How about if I help you with that?"

He looked at this twenty-three-year-old pastor and said, "Sure, why don't you help me with that."

I suggested we start with a basic résumé. I wrote down his name. When I asked for his contact information, he said, "Dude, I don't have a phone. I don't have an address."

So we skipped that. I moved on to ask about his education and found out that it was very limited.

I asked for his references. "If I had references," he said, "I wouldn't be out here on the street."

"Well," I said, "why don't we just look at the classified ads and see what we can find that you might be qualified for."

What I really found, after an hour and a half sitting with this man, was how little I knew about the situations in which many homeless people find themselves. Certainly, we all should do what we can to support ourselves. But sometimes people face challenges they don't know how to overcome on their own, or they simply don't have the resources to do it. Our calling is not to shrug off responsibility for helping our neighbors by invoking that phrase, "God helps those who help themselves." Instead, God commands his people to take special concern for the poor, the orphan, the widow, and the needy.

That's the message we read in Leviticus 23:22. God says, "When you harvest your land's produce, you must not harvest all the way to the edge of your field; and don't gather every remaining bit of your harvest. Leave these items for the poor and the immigrant; I am the LORD your God." That is a serious command. God insisted that farmers intentionally leave part of their crop on their property unharvested. Instead of consuming it themselves or selling it, this portion was to be left for those who were not able to make ends meet or for the strangers in the land. The command involved compassion and charity but also the dignity of work: the poor could harvest a portion for themselves. And it involved recognition that God is the ultimate source of wealth and property. God is essentially saying, "You're not being required to share your wealth, because the fields were not yours to begin with. They ultimately belong to me. My commandment to leave part of the field unharvested is my strategy for making sure my people who are struggling have enough."

In Scripture, God consistently calls us to help those who cannot help themselves, or those who require help before they can help themselves.

- James writes these familiar words in the New Testament: "True devotion, the kind that is pure and faultless before God the Father, is this: to care for orphans and widows in their difficulties" (James 1:27).
- In the Parable of the Sheep and Goats (Matthew 25) and the Parable of the Good Samaritan (Luke 10), Jesus tells us that God judges us not only by our faith, but by whether our faith led us to a greater compassion for the poor and needy.
- Paul says that we are saved by the kind of faith that moves our hearts to action—"faith working through love" (Galatians 5:6).
- Proverbs captures the twin ideas of *ora et labora*. In Proverbs 10:4, the author writes, "Laziness brings poverty; hard work makes

one rich." Then Proverbs 19:17 adds, "Those who are gracious to the poor lend to the LORD, and the LORD will fully repay them." Elsewhere in Proverbs you'll find these verses of wisdom: "Those who close their ears to the cries of the poor will themselves call out but receive no answer" (21:13) and "Happy are generous people, because they give some of their food to the poor" (22:9).

- The Bible even suggests that compassion for others is a form of worshiping and being obedient to God. Speaking on God's behalf, the prophet Hosea writes, "I desire faithful love and not sacrifice" (Hosea 6:6). Jesus quotes this verse to the Pharisees and urges them to go and study carefully what it means.

In a very real and immediate sense, the biblical truth—in contrast to the half truth—is that God helps those who *can't* help themselves. Showing compassion and mercy for those who struggle is part of the very character of God.

In my experience, God typically meets the needs of those who are poor or struggling or hurting by acting through other people. I haven't directly observed God sending angels to bring food, clothing, and shelter down from heaven. What I have experienced is the way God puts it on our hearts and on the hearts of others to help. We can (and should) debate the best ways of helping and not hurting, of creating independence and not dependence. What is not debatable is our calling to help. People who think they are Christian and yet have no compassion for those in need and do little to care for them, believing "God only helps those who help themselves," have missed an essential component of the gospel.

People who think they are Christian and yet have no compassion for those in need and do little to care for them, believing "God only helps those who help themselves," have missed an essential component of the gospel.

One day after church, around Christmastime, a member of our congregation who was unemployed told me that he had received an envelope with no name or return address on it. When he opened the envelope, he found a hundred dollar bill. As he told me the story, tears welled up in his eyes. "Pastor," he said, "you have no idea what that meant. I felt that God was speaking to me, and helping me, through someone here at our church. I knew at that moment that God had not forgotten me."

In a similar vein, I recall watching a scene unfold in a hotel some years ago as a woman attempted to check in. When she presented her credit card, the clerk processed it but informed her that the card had been refused. The woman was distraught. She did not know what she was going to do or where she could stay.

The woman walked away from the desk, thinking she could use her phone to call someone who might be able to help, and told the clerk she would come back. After she was out of earshot, the man who had been standing behind her in line and had witnessed the situation stepped up. He told the clerk that he wanted to pay for the woman's room for the night.

"When she comes back," the man said, "please don't tell her who paid. Just tell her it was a gift from God."

At our church, a portion of the offerings we receive during the year help support a number of outside ministries. But for our services on Christmas Eve, we give away the entire amount. We challenge our members to give an amount equal to what they spend on their own family at Christmas in an offering that benefits children in poverty.* In a typical year this will be many times a regular offering. Some of the special offering has gone to provide beds, blankets, and books for children in Kansas City. Some has built medical clinics and clean-water wells in Africa. Some has funded schools in Honduras. Our members give because they believe God works through people to help those who cannot do these things on their own. It is through such acts that the lives of the helpers and the helped are forever changed. And in this way Christians work to change the world in God's name.

God's Help for the Helpless = Grace

There is a second sense in which, thankfully, the idea that God helps those who help themselves does not capture the truth of the Bible. Sometimes we can't help ourselves, not because we are poor or destitute or

---

* We were inspired in this idea several years ago by my friend Mike Slaughter and the Ginghamsburg Church in Tipp City, Ohio.

without resources but because we have descended too deeply into sin or despair.

God is the God of the hopeless cause, the God who loves sinners, the God who walks with us through the darkest valleys. He is the God who brings light into our darkness and helps us find peace amid our times of anxiety and despair. God rescues, redeems, and forgives. We receive blessings from God even though we cannot earn them and don't deserve them. Even when we have made a mess of things and can't fix them, God extends mercy to us. There's a word for God's mercy toward those who cannot help themselves. We call it grace.

There are many kinds of help we need in life. One involves the basics of life: food, shelter, clothing, security, health care. If you took a psychology class in high school or college, these essentials were outlined in Maslow's Hierarchy of Needs. God meets these physical needs through our own work and through community, when we and others act as our brothers' and sisters' keepers.

But as Maslow recognized, there are also needs of a higher order. Besides basic physical needs, we need acceptance, love, and a sense of belonging. We need hope, peace, comfort, forgiveness, and interior strength. We need to know that our lives have worth. We need an understanding of our purpose in life so that we can pursue it and be fulfilled. Many of these needs might be thought of as spiritual or existential needs. They may be met by other people, but often they are met by God's gracious work in our lives.

The week before I wrote these words, I met with a grieving couple. They are longtime members of our church, and they volunteer in our congregational care ministry, visiting and providing comfort to others who are experiencing a loss. Now they were experiencing a loss of their own: the death of their thirty-four-year-old son. They told me they didn't know how people made it through such a time without faith, without knowing they would see their child again one day. But even with faith it was difficult. The couple told me they felt God's presence and grace carrying them through the terrible loss. They were also amazed by the ways God's people in their church family had surrounded them with love and sustained them.

Three days before I talked to this grieving couple, I met with a mother who had lost her teenaged son earlier in the year. She told me how, in the dark days following his death, she essentially had stopped functioning. "I felt like a building had fallen on me," she said. "I couldn't breathe. I couldn't eat. I couldn't take care of myself. I couldn't even dress myself. I was like a little child."

She told me that two things had sustained her through the hardest moments. When she couldn't eat, her friends and church family brought her food and made her take nourishment. When she couldn't get out of her pajamas in the morning, her girlfriends helped her get dressed and meet the day. When she could not help herself, God worked through others to help her.

But she also felt God's hand directly. In the depth of her grief, and even now, she heard God whisper to her, "He's safe with me. He's in my arms. You don't have to be afraid." As she confronted that higher level of needs, she found that her faith in God, and God's work in her life, had saved her.

When I think of what these people experienced, I hear the words of the psalmist: "In my distress I called upon the LORD; to my God I cried for help. From his temple he heard my voice, and my cry to him reached his ears.... He reached down from on high, he took me; he drew me out of mighty waters" (Psalm 18:6, 16 NRSV).

I think of a man who spent most of his life living for himself, for wealth, and affirmation from others. He was driven to succeed. But that quality led him to be away from his family and uninvolved in their lives. It also led him to drink. Over time, he became helpless to control his craving for alcohol. As a consequence, he lost the job that mattered so much to him, and he nearly lost his family. When it seemed there was nowhere else to turn, he turned to God. Though he did not deserve it, and could not earn it, he felt God's mercy and forgiveness. He turned his life over to God, asked for God's mercy and grace, and found in God a second chance and a new beginning.

I think of a couple who came to one of our pastors at a time of great distress. Through their tears the husband related how, in his constant business travel, he had found himself watching Internet pornography, which eventually resulted in his calling a woman to his hotel room for sex. This began to be a pattern in his life.

When his wife eventually found out, it shattered her world. The husband came to his senses. He did not want their marriage to fail, but by that time he was at the bottom of a deep pit he had dug for himself. He wondered if there was any hope for someone like him—someone who knew that, by all rights, he didn't deserve forgiveness and grace. The wife wondered whether she could find healing. Both feared that their marriage could not be saved.

They met with one of our pastors, a wonderful counselor through whom God works. She told the husband that there was always hope if he turned his life back toward Christ, because Christ is in the business of redeeming those who are broken, whether or not they deserve it. She told the couple she did not know if their marriage could be saved. But she thought it was possible if both of them were willing to pray and work at it—*ora et labora*.

The couple are still married today, many years later. They found joy again in their lives. They were willing to work to help themselves. But they also trusted in faith, and that faith helped them move forward. The beginning of their journey back toward wholeness was to trust that God would help them along the road when their own efforts might not be enough. It seems almost impossible to me that the kind of deep forgiveness and healing they experienced—a degree of healing that was hard to imagine that day when they met in our pastor's office—would ever have happened without the help of God.

Another member of our church recently wrote me a note that conveyed this same understanding. "I tried 'helping' myself for most of forty-five years," he wrote. "It wasn't until I surrendered to the fact that I am powerless that God gave me strength to overcome."

I think of a woman who feels unloved and worthless. To her God says, "You are my beloved child! You matter to me! Trust me and walk in my love." And when she does, everything changes. It's the same for all of us. In God's willingness to help us when we don't deserve it, we discover grace.

Grace is not something we earn, buy, or work for. We cannot help ourselves into grace. We can only ask for and accept it.

Once again I remember the words of the psalmist: "I lift up my eyes to the hills—from where will my help come? My help comes from the LORD, who made heaven and earth" (Psalm 121:1-2 NRSV). How comforting it is to know that God is our help in times of trouble, that God is gracious and merciful.

This concept of grace is central to the Christian gospel. It is the *undeserved* work of God in our lives, the unmerited favor of God. Grace is not something we earn, buy, or work for. We cannot help ourselves into grace. We can only ask for and accept it. The essence of grace is that *God helps those who cannot help themselves*!

"I Am Here"

There are times when we can help ourselves, and we should. God is counting on us to do the best we can—to pray and to work. There are times when people cannot make it on their own, and God prompts us to help. We become the hands of God. We become God's answer to someone else's prayer, God's instruments of grace.

But you will find, if you haven't already, that a time will come when you cannot help yourself. There are things from which you simply cannot save yourself, no matter how hard you try. You will not have the strength or the resources or the knowledge. And there may be times when you don't believe you deserve help because you know you are responsible for the difficult situation in which you find yourself.

In those moments we cry out to God, the only one who can help us. And despite the fact that we are poor and pitiable, weak and afraid, and that we have made a mess of things, God reaches out and picks us up and makes us clean. God says, "I love you and will not abandon you. Put your trust in me. Together we can make this right."

This is the message from God that we find over and over again in Scripture. "I am here," says God. "You matter to me. Your life has meaning. Nothing, no matter what you may have done or been unable to do, can separate you from my love."

That is what we call grace.

Thanks be to God who helps those who work and pray. And, even more, thanks be to God who helps those (like all of us, sometimes) who cannot help themselves.

God, thank you for grace. Thank you for the many times you have helped me when I did not deserve it. Thank you for your love. Thank you for your forgiveness. Thank you for the meaning you bring to my life. Thank you for rescuing me. Please use me, Lord, as your instrument to help others who are in need. I offer myself to you. In Jesus' name. Amen.

3.

GOD WON'T GIVE YOU MORE THAN YOU CAN HANDLE

No temptation has seized you that isn't common for people. But God is faithful. He won't allow you to be tempted beyond your abilities. Instead, with the temptation, God will also supply a way out so that you will be able to endure it.

—1 Corinthians 10:13

God is our refuge and strength, a help always near in times of great trouble. That's why we won't be afraid when the world falls apart.

—Psalm 46:1-2

3.

GOD WON'T GIVE YOU MORE THAN YOU CAN HANDLE

"I know you're going through a tough time right now. You feel like you're sinking. The burden is too heavy. You don't know how much more you can bear. But it's going to be all right. You're going to make it through. Remember, God never gives us more than we can handle."

I suspect every Christian has heard some variation on those words before. Perhaps someone has said them to you when you were in the midst of a trying time. Perhaps you have said them to someone else.

Undoubtedly, people mean well when they say those words. They mean to encourage and strengthen others. They certainly don't intend to place obstacles in the path of someone's faith. And at times, words such as this may in fact bring comfort.

Yet the idea that God won't give us more than we can handle is another of those biblical half truths that we often accept and repeat without giving them much thought. It's an idea we really need to reflect upon carefully before using it to encourage someone. We need to consider where this statement may go wrong and then search for the whole truth behind the half truth.

Context and Origin

Like many spiritual half truths, this one has some scriptural basis. People usually cite 1 Corinthians 10:13 as the source for this idea, and usually it is paraphrased (or I think, more accurately, it is misquoted) as "God won't give you more than you can handle." Listen again to what Paul actually writes: "No temptation has seized you that isn't common for people. But God is faithful. He won't allow you to be tempted beyond your abilities. Instead, with the temptation, God will also supply a way out so that you will be able to endure it."

Some point out that the Greek word Paul uses for "tempted" in this passage is *peirasmos,* which can mean "tested." They suggest that "tested" is what Paul has in mind, so that the passage might in fact be saying, "He won't give you more than you can handle." But a look at the context of Paul's words shows that he was talking about temptation, including sexual immorality (v. 8) and idolatry (v. 14) but not trials and hardships.

Paul is writing here to the Christian community at Corinth, a large port city in Greece. Around A.D. 51, during one of his missionary journeys, Paul founded a church there. Corinth was like many port towns: people and influences from all over the world were on display there. Pagan influences were everywhere. I have been to Corinth, have walked its streets, and have seen some of the dozen or more temples that stood in Paul's day. They were on nearly every corner. If you purchased meat in the local marketplace, chances were good that it came from an animal that had been sacrificed to a pagan god at one of Corinth's temples. Such was Corinth's reputation in the Roman world that "to live like a Corinthian," a phrase popular at the time, was synonymous with drunkenness and sexual license.

Most of the newly minted Christians Paul was addressing had been pagans until the church was founded. They were trying to leave behind the idol worship and the temple prostitutes that were part of religious life in places like Corinth's shrine to Aphrodite, the Greek goddess of love. And yet these Christians still lived in a city where they were surrounded by sexual immorality. Temptation was everywhere, and it was bound to be strong among those who had spent most of their lives immersed in pagan practices. They were trying to follow Jesus, but some of them also were going back to their former ways, and Paul was trying to help them.

And so the context for this verse in 1 Corinthians is self-discipline in the face of temptation with the hope of avoiding sin, particularly the sins of sexual immorality and idolatry. Paul reminds the Corinthians that they are not the only ones who have dealt with these challenges. When the children of Israel were in the wilderness, Paul says, they too gave in to idol worship and sexual immorality, then had to face the adverse consequences of their actions. Paul describes how God struck down the Israelites because of their sin.

> These things happened to them as an example and were written as a warning for us....Don't worship false gods like some of [the Israelites] did....So those who think they are standing need to watch out or else they may fall. No temptation has seized you that isn't common for people. But God is faithful. He won't allow you to be tempted beyond your abilities. Instead, with the temptation, God will also supply a way out so that you will be able to endure it.
>
> (1 Corinthians 10:11, 7, 12-13)

Paul is telling the Corinthian Christians that their experience is not unique. Just as the Israelites were tempted, so too the Corinthians will be (and were being) tempted.

In fact, we'll all be tempted. Jesus himself experienced temptation. This passage is not about God declining to give you more burdens in life than you can handle. It is about God helping you when you are tempted. Again, the Greek word for *tempted* can mean "tested." Temptation is indeed a test of your resolve, your character, and your faith. And that is what Paul is talking about here—not about adversity and the difficult circumstances that come into every life at some point.

The good news, according to Paul, is that God will not allow us to be tempted beyond our abilities. Instead, God will always supply us with a way out so that we can endure the temptation.

Looking for a Way Out of Temptation—or Not

My own experience is that when I'm tempted, there is always a way out. The problem is that I may not be looking very hard for the exit.

As I write this, I have been making a conscious effort to exercise more and cut back a little on what I eat. The other day I left my office to walk to lunch. I planned on eating something light. I picked up half a sandwich and was walking back to the office (where, as it happened, I was writing a sermon on temptation). In the hallway I ran into Joan, who directs our congregation's café program that coordinates meals for different groups that use the church. She was pushing a cart with bags of leftovers from Dairy Queen.

Having spent several hours working on my sermon about temptation, you might think I would have simply greeted Joan and walked on to my office to eat my low-calorie, low-fat sandwich while continuing to work on my sermon. Of course, I did no such thing. With my half sandwich in hand, I asked Joan, "Hey, what's in those DQ sacks?" She told me they were leftovers from a lunch meeting. I should have said, "Great, thanks, Joan. Have a great day!" But instead I pressed further: "What kind of leftovers?" As it turned out, the bags were filled with things I love: hamburgers, hot dogs, and chicken strips with white cream gravy and fries.

I asked Joan, "So, what are you doing with these leftovers?" She said, "I was just going to see if anyone wanted them. Would you like a lunch?" I went for the box of chicken strips, cream gravy, and fries. And did I stop there? No, I saw that Joan's cart carried several other bags, so I had to ask about them too. They contained ice cream sandwiches and sundaes. I took one of those too. All while having spent the morning working on a sermon on temptation! What a dope!

Temptation inevitably comes our way. On that day, it came to me on a rolling cart with DQ treats. But in my experience, it isn't God who tempts us. We do a pretty good job of that all by ourselves. In fact, Scripture says, "God is not tempted by any form of evil, nor does he tempt anyone" (James 1:13).

Some might point to the Lord's Prayer to refute that statement, where we ask God, "Lead us not into temptation" (KJV). However, I maintain that the emphasis is on *lead us*, as in "Please, God, lead us— not into temptation, as we would lead ourselves—but onto the right path. And deliver us from the evil one."

The problem isn't that God fails to provide a way out of temptation; it's that when a way appears, we usually don't pursue it. In fact, we often hear the Spirit's voice trying to lead us away from something we shouldn't do. When I reflect on it, it's almost humorous sometimes how God tries to put up speed bumps on the road to temptation and we bounce right over them. Surely we lead ourselves into temptation.

The problem isn't that God fails to provide a way out of temptation; it's that when a way appears, we usually don't pursue it.

By the way, I've found that perhaps dogs also need help with temptation. We have a fifteen-year-old beagle named Maggie. One day we let her outside and apparently left the garage door open. Inside the garage was a brand-new twenty-pound bag of dog food that had not been opened yet. Maggie's well-developed sense of smell—it turns out that dogs have millions more sensory receptors in their noses than humans do—led her right to the bag. She tore open the top and for the next ten to fifteen minutes proceeded to eat as much as she could before coming back into the house. God didn't lead her into temptation; Maggie's nose and stomach did that. The next day, when we discovered the ripped-open bag, we also discovered that Maggie had eaten so much and so fast that she had made herself sick!

When it comes to temptation, humans are not so different from dogs. When we give into temptation and choose a direction God doesn't want us to go, we also make ourselves sick. Oh, Lord, lead us—not into temptation.

As we carefully examine the context of 1 Corinthians 10:13, we discover it's not about whether God will give us more than we can handle. Neither is it about whether God will lead us into greater temptation than we can handle. Instead, Paul is saying that *when* we are tempted—as, inevitably, we sometimes will be—God will make sure the temptations are not so strong that we can't resist them. God will give us a way out of temptation, if only we are alert to it and will seize it.

That's a helpful promise. The devil can't make you do anything! Resistance is not futile. You *can* overcome temptation.

Where This Half Truth Misses the Mark

So, even if Scripture doesn't support the saying, is it still true that "God won't give you more than you can handle"? After all, many believe this idea is helpful for people going through hardship or facing adversity. They offer it as encouragement to others who are struggling or who feel overwhelmed—as in:

> "I know your life is hard right now, but God won't give you more than you can handle. Be encouraged!"

> "I know you've lost a friend (experienced adversity at work / been sick / are financially struggling), but don't worry. God won't give you more pain and suffering than you can bear."

I remember a conversation on this subject with a woman who told me, "For years this statement helped me when I was facing difficult things. I kept telling myself that God wouldn't give me more than I could handle. It reassured me that somehow I was going to make it through. Then one day I was at my therapist's office and mentioned it to him. He laughed and said, 'Are you kidding me? Surely you don't really believe that. I can tell you plenty of stories about people who had more than they could handle. In fact, my profession consists of helping just such people.'"

The counselor reminded the woman that in her own case, she had come to him because the emotional pain and difficulty she was facing had been more than she could handle. In addition, the woman's mother had committed suicide because life had become more difficult than she could handle.

At first, the woman was angry that her therapist had called her belief into question. But the more she reflected on their conversation, the more she concluded that he was right. Maybe sometimes we face situations that truly are more than we can handle, and that's why we turn to others for help.

Let's take a few minutes to look again at this commonly recited statement and consider why we may not want to share it with others when they are wrestling with adversity.

God Won't Give You...

Let's start with the first four words: "God won't give you...." When we say those words, we are implying that whatever difficult or painful things are happening in your life, God gave them to you.

As I argued in Chapter 1, Christians should think twice before suggesting that God wills bad things to happen to us. The same argument applies here. So the first problem with the idea that God won't give us more than we can handle is that, in my view, God doesn't give us bad things to handle. Otherwise it would be like saying, "God *gave* you this horrible, painful, hurtful thing—but he'll stop giving you more suffering before you reach your breaking point, so don't worry!"

Recently I traveled to the African nation of Malawi. I've been there on a couple of occasions as our church has been in partnership with the Methodist churches there. Traveling with a videographer and our director of missions, we were going to see the work we'd done together with the churches there to bring clean water to villages and to support projects benefiting orphans. We were also looking at ways we might partner with our Malawian brothers and sisters in the future.

Malawi is a country filled with wonderful people, but it is also a nation where so many live on so very little. Its people routinely face very challenging circumstances. When you are already struggling in this way, it's all the more difficult to deal with a burden like a natural disaster. But that is what happened to Malawi the week before we were scheduled to arrive. The country came under torrential rains that resulted in widespread flooding. The southern half of the country was declared a disaster zone. The floods wiped out most of the crops just as harvest season was approaching—meaning that people who already had barely enough to eat would have even less without emergency food assistance. Hundreds of people were killed in the flooding, hundreds more were missing, and approximately two hundred thousand others were displaced from their homes. On top of everything else, the country faced a deadly outbreak of cholera.

Needless to say, I didn't tell those suffering people, "Don't worry, God won't give you more than you can handle." Rather, I said, "How can we help?"

After returning to Kansas City I preached a sermon on the theme of this chapter. Apparently it struck a chord, because I received the following note from a woman in the congregation:

> In response to your question about God not giving us more than we can handle...if someone tells me this one more time, I may lose it. First of all, God didn't cause my husband to beat me, he didn't make my brother commit suicide, he didn't plant the IED that my nephew hit, which will result in him losing his leg, and he didn't give my best friend cancer. I could go on, but you get the idea.

She was right. When people had tried to encourage her with this phrase, she heard them saying that God had given her all these things, but he would likely stop now because he knew she couldn't handle any more. What kind of God tests his children by having their spouses beat them, their siblings take their lives, and their friends suffer from cancer?

We will face adversity in our lives. We will experience hardships. We, or someone we love, may face terminal illness. We may struggle with debilitating depression or suicidal thoughts or grief so heavy that we feel we'll suffocate. We may walk through financial circumstances where it seems there is no way out. If we are like most human beings, at some point we absolutely will face things that are more than we can handle.

The promise of Scripture is not that we won't go through hard times. . . . What Scripture does promise is that at all times, good or bad, God wants to be our help and our strength.

Those things are not part of God's perfect plan. They are not sent by God. But they are part of the human experience. I don't believe God gives them, but I trust that God walks with us through them—in fact God, in the person of Jesus, has already walked through our shared human experience with us. He knew what it was to suffer and to face rejection, betrayal, torture, and death. And his resurrection proclaims that evil, hate, pain, and death itself will not have the final word in our lives.

The promise of Scripture is not that we won't go through hard times. It is not that we can handle by ourselves everything that life throws our way. What Scripture does promise is that at all times, good or bad, God wants to be our help and our strength. And so, in the words of Peter, "Throw all your anxiety onto him, because he cares about you" (1 Peter 5:7).

A Better Promise

If we can move beyond the half truth and scrub it from our vocabulary, let me suggest a promise that is truer, more accurate, and more scriptural, one that many Christians have already figured out. It's not that God won't give you more than you can handle, but that *God will help you handle all that you've been given.*

This revised statement doesn't sound so terribly different from the original, but the theological difference is striking. "God will help you handle all that you've been given" does not suggest that the struggles and suffering in your life were given to you by God, or that he will load you with burdens but will stop just short of your breaking point. The statement doesn't suggest that suffering is "given" to you by God at all. Instead, it acknowledges that adversity happens in life, and it promises that when you go through trials and tribulations, God walks with you through it all.*

This scriptural truth is expressed beautifully by the psalmist: "Yea, though I walk through the valley of the shadow of death, I will fear no evil: for thou art with me" (Psalm 23:4 KJV). The psalmist presumes he will walk through the darkest valley. He doesn't expect God to keep it from happening, but he takes comfort in knowing that he will not be alone.

Several years ago I went to visit a woman in a psychiatric hospital. Her son had taken his own life, and she had witnessed it. When I entered her hospital room, I found her in the fetal position, hardly able to communicate. I wrapped my arms around her and told her, "I love you, and God loves you. I am so sorry. This was not God's will for your life or for your son." We held hands, and we talked about God's ability to see her through that terrible time. I affirmed the words of the psalmist: "God is our refuge and strength, a help always near in times of great trouble.

---

* Some object that even this phrase points to hardship being "given to us" but its wording, to me, points to adversity coming from life itself or from illness or other people. Perhaps better is the idea that God will help us handle all that comes our way.

That's why we won't be afraid when the world falls apart, when the mountains crumble into the center of the sea" (Psalm 46:1-2).

I knew the woman probably couldn't process all the things we discussed during my visit, but I tried to tell her that God understands when people feel so overwhelmed that they consider suicide. I told her that I believe that God's grace extended to her son even in that desperate act, and that, even though it might seem she could never move past it, God would carry her through.

Recently, three years after her son's death, I saw a note the woman posted on Facebook. In it, she described how she had survived that terrible trauma with the help of God, the church family, and her "stretcher-bearers," those people who carried her when she could not walk on her own. She wrote that she had begun to find joy in her life again—joy and hope.

During the twenty-five years I have served as pastor at Church of the Resurrection, I have walked through difficult times with many members of the congregation. I have sometimes wondered, as I did with the woman whose son had taken his own life, whether the people would be able to make it through those times. But my years of pastoral ministry have taught me that people find strength to survive the worst times and experiences, and that some of the most important resources they have are their faith in God, their experience of God, and God's care for them. Watching them, I have learned to trust in God even more completely.

My trust in God is not that he won't give me more than I can bear, because I don't believe he's the one who would give those things. It is not that God is testing me by bringing bad things into my life. Instead, I trust that when bad things happen during the course of life, God will sustain me, walk with me, hold me near, comfort and care for me. I can talk with God even if I can't see him. He is as close as the air I breathe. Though I might experience the pain of a traumatic event, I maintain faith that, at some point, joy will overshadow the pain. I have witnessed it time and again, watching members of our congregation go through situations I could only describe as hell on earth, then move past those situations with help from God and from the people God brought into their lives.

I trust that when bad things happen during the course of life, God will sustain me, walk with me, hold me near, comfort and care for me.

The prophet Zechariah once described his fellow Israelites as "prisoners of hope" (Zechariah 9:12). I love that phrase, because it expresses our faith as people who trust in God. It is this faith that Paul captured well for the Christians at Rome, Christians who would one day face persecution for their faith. Paul wrote,

> Who will separate us from Christ's love? Will we be separated by trouble, or distress, or harassment, or famine, or nakedness, or danger, or sword?...But in all these things we win a sweeping victory through the one who loved us. I'm convinced that nothing can separate us from God's love in Christ Jesus our Lord: not death or life, not angels or rulers, not present things or future things, not powers or height or depth, or any other thing that is created. (Romans 8:35, 37-39)

Several pages back, I shared with you a note I received from a woman whose husband had abused her, whose brother had committed suicide, and whose nephew had lost a leg. She wrote that she would lose it if one more person said to her, "God won't give you more than you can handle." In her note, she went on to express her faith in the midst of challenging times:

> I absolutely reject the idea that all of these horrible things...were God's will. What I do know, beyond a shadow of a doubt, is that he is helping me cope. It's not easy, but I know that I am never alone, even if it feels that way sometimes. I know I can turn to God and cry and kick and scream, and he will comfort me. I can thank him for connecting me with the attorney who helped me out of an abusive marriage. I can thank him for giving me the strength to talk about my brother's suicide in the hopes that it might be helpful to someone else. I can thank him for allowing my nephew to live instead of die. God is turning the challenges and using them for good.

This was the same conclusion reached by a woman named Annie Johnson Flint more than a century ago. Annie was born on Christmas Eve 1866 in a small New Jersey town. At the age of three she lost her mother. Soon after that, her father became so ill that he could no longer take care of his children and was forced to give them up for adoption. Annie was fortunate to be taken in by a wonderful, loving family named Flint. But before she finished high school, both her adoptive parents had died as well. Imagine losing not just one set but two sets of parents as a child.

Annie longed to be a teacher, continued her education, and achieved her goal. But not long after she began teaching, she was diagnosed with a degenerative disease that left her unable to walk or to live independently. She spent the rest of her life, roughly another forty years, bound to a wheelchair and living in a sanitarium where others could provide for her physical needs.

Annie's condition meant the end of her teaching career. Instead, she began writing poetry, an interest she had developed during her childhood with the Flints. Over the years she wrote a number of popular religious poems. As time went by, her illness caused the joints in her hands to swell so painfully that it was difficult to write, so she began dictating her poems. She noted that she wrote not to fulfill her own need to express ideas but in the hope of helping others who were undergoing the kind of challenges with which she was so familiar.

Annie is perhaps best remembered for a poem she wrote called "What God Hath Promised."

> God hath not promised skies always blue,
> Flower strewn pathways all our lives through;
> God hath not promised sun without rain,
> Joy without sorrow, peace without pain.
>
> But God hath promised strength for the day,
> Rest for the labor, light for the way,
> Grace for the trials, help from above,
> Unfailing sympathy, undying love.

When you're facing temptation, by all means turn to 1 Corinthians 10:13. In reading it, remember that God will help you find a way through the temptation, if you will open yourself to the opportunity.

But when you're walking through hard times, it's all right to admit, "I can't handle this by myself, and I need help." At times we need a doctor or therapist to help us. More often, we need family, friends, neighbors, pastors, and brothers and sisters in our church family who come alongside us to carry us through our adversity. And we turn to God, trusting that God walks with us, that God's Spirit is at work in us and in our life situations, helping us handle all that life gives us.

O God, how grateful we are for the way you walk with us in every moment of our lives. In those moments when we're tempted and tested, help us remember that we can resist and that you make a way out of temptation. You give us the strength we need when we turn to you. Lead us, not into temptation as we would go, but in your path and away from evil.

When we walk through difficulty and adversity, help us remember that these burdens did not come from you, but that you have said you would help us bear them. Thank you for people who come along our path and help carry us through those challenging times. Help us have eyes to see those around us who need your help—and to see how we might be instruments of your help for them. How grateful we are, O God, that you are our refuge and strength, an ever-present help in times of trouble. Therefore we will not fear, even when our world seems to be falling apart. Amen.

4.

GOD SAID IT, I BELIEVE IT, THAT SETTLES IT

You shall have a designated area outside the camp to which you shall go. With your utensils you shall have a trowel; when you relieve yourself outside, you shall dig a hole with it and then cover up your excrement. Because the LORD your God travels along with your camp, to save you and to hand over your enemies to you, therefore your camp must be holy, so that he may not see anything indecent among you and turn away from you.

—Deuteronomy 23:12-14 NRSV

4.

GOD SAID IT, I BELIEVE IT, THAT SETTLES IT

"God said it, I believe it, that settles it." Do a quick Google search, and you'll find hundreds of thousands of web pages offering this slogan. You can put it on a bumper sticker, find it on billboards, and listen to it in gospel songs from the 1970s. The slogan has had a long and abundant life.

Some have even taken it a step further, amending the statement to read: "God said it, that settles it, whether I believe it or not."

There's nothing necessarily wrong with a theological statement that's short enough to put on a bumper sticker. For example, "God loves you" is sound bumper-sticker theology.

So, what could possibly be wrong with the statement? Like other half truths, this one certainly sounds right. If God says something, of course we should believe it. If we had a question, and the angel of God stood before us and told us God's answer, that would indeed settle the matter.

Of course, what Christians generally mean by "God said it" is that the Bible says it, therefore they believe it, and that settles it. And that, too, seems right. If the Bible says something, we believe it as Christians, and that settles it, right?

What could possibly be only half true about this statement concerning Scripture? The challenge is that it oversimplifies Scripture. If we strictly adhere to a "God says it, I believe it, that settles it" approach to the Bible, we can find ourselves setting all kinds of unusual limits on our behavior, even down to where believers are allowed to go to the bathroom.

The Bible on Where to Go to the Bathroom

I'll venture a guess that you have never heard a sermon preached or read a devotional on the passage from Deuteronomy that's shown at the beginning of this chapter. Let's look at it again.

> You shall have a designated area outside the camp to which you shall go. With your utensils you shall have a trowel; when you relieve yourself outside, you shall dig a hole with it and then cover up your excrement. Because the LORD your God travels along with your camp, to save you and to hand over your enemies to you, therefore your camp must be holy, so that he may not see anything indecent among you and turn away from you. (Deuteronomy 23:12-14 NRSV)

If you happened to be 140 years old, you might have heard a few sermons on this text. In the 1880s, believe it or not, you could find preachers expounding on the biblical teaching in Deuteronomy 23 about where to relieve oneself.

Why? Because in the 1880s, indoor plumbing was becoming widely available for the first time, and churches were beginning to debate its merits. Before that time, if someone felt "nature's call" while they were at church, they had to leave the building and visit an outhouse. Suddenly, parishioners all over America began suggesting that everyone would benefit if they modernized their churches with indoor plumbing.

No one today suggests that churches should build outhouses. You won't find a church built in the past seventy-five years that lacks indoor toilets. In fact, when congregations plan new buildings, one of the top questions members ask is "How many toilets will the new building have?"

But in the 1880s, when indoor plumbing was an innovation, that passage from Deuteronomy was taken by many to mean that God was against indoor plumbing. The argument against bathrooms in the building went something like this:

When the Israelites were in the wilderness before coming into the Promised Land, the Lord was with them in their camps as they traveled. God made his residence in their midst. So, according to the instructions in Deuteronomy, the Israelites were to set up an area outside their encampments for relieving themselves. That way, the Lord would not see anything "indecent" among them. The passage explicitly says that God might "turn away" from the Israelites— that is, God might deny his blessings and protection for the people—if he saw something indecent. And it suggests that human excrement, though part of the natural workings of the human bodies that God designed, is somehow unholy and should not be allowed in God's camp.

By this logic, since churches were understood as God's house—places, like the Israelite encampments in the wilderness, where God was with the people— then the same rules about where people could relieve themselves must apply. An outhouse was, literally, outside the church, whereas indoor plumbing brought toilets inside God's house. So it was not unreasonable, based on that text about a very different time and place, to argue that God would find it unholy and indecent for believers to go to the bathroom inside God's house. And in fact many preachers made that argument from the pulpit. God said it, I believe it, that settles it.

And though it may seem extreme by our modern way of looking at it, this commandment in Deuteronomy is far from the only challenging passage in Scripture. *

Going to Extremes

If we really are serious about a "God says it, I believe it, that settles it" approach to the Bible, here are some ways many of us would need to alter our lives:

---

* For a much more comprehensive look at Scripture, please see my book *Making Sense of the Bible* (HarperOne, 2014).

- Don't wear blended fabrics or sow two
  different seeds in your fields.
  (Leviticus 19:19)
- Eliminate pork and shrimp from your diet.
  (Leviticus 11:7-12)
- For men, don't trim the edges of your beard.
  (Leviticus 19:27)
- Children who curse or strike their parents
  or who are persistently rebellious should
  be put to death. (Exodus 21:15 and
  Deuteronomy 21:18-21)
- Don't mow your yard or clean your house
  on Saturdays (the Sabbath), or you can be
  put to death. (Exodus 35:2)
- For women, if you're not a virgin when you
  marry, the men of your town are to stone
  you to death. (Deuteronomy 22:21)

A couple of years ago I received a Facebook message from a teenager in my congregation. He wanted a tattoo, but his father, quoting Leviticus 19:28, would not allow it. So the young man looked up the passage and found that the verse before it includes rules for men's hair and beards. He cited Scripture back to his

GOD SAID IT, I BELIEVE IT, THAT SETTLES IT

father to remind him that getting a haircut—at least if it involved cutting the hair on the side of his head—was also forbidden.

Most of us have not read the Old Testament passages listed above and said, "God said it, I believe it, that settles it." Instead the typical Christian response is that these Old Testament verses reflect God's covenant with Israel but are no longer binding upon Christians. Yet Jesus said in Matthew 5:17-20,

> "Don't even begin to think that I have come to do away with the Law and the Prophets. I haven't come to do away with them but to fulfill them. I say to you very seriously that as long as heaven and earth exist, neither the smallest letter nor even the smallest stroke of a pen will be erased from the Law until everything there becomes a reality. Therefore, whoever ignores one of the least of these commands and teaches others to do the same will be called the lowest in the kingdom of heaven. But whoever keeps these commands and teaches people to keep them will be called great in the kingdom of heaven. I say to you that unless your righteousness is greater than the righteousness of the legal experts and the Pharisees, you will never enter the kingdom of heaven."

Even Jesus, however, did not interpret the Law in a "God said it, I believe it, that settles it" kind of way. He had a very liberal interpretation of the Sabbath laws, quite different from how those laws were applied by Moses when he had a man put to death for picking up sticks on the Sabbath. Jesus noted, "The Sabbath was created for humans; humans weren't created for the Sabbath" (Mark 2:27).

Even Jesus did not interpret the Law in a "God said it, I believe it, that settles it" kind of way.

When it came to divorce, Jesus actually was more conservative than the Law. In Matthew 19:3 he was asked about the portion of the Law that allowed men to divorce their wives by issuing a certificate of divorce (Deuteronomy 24:1-4). Jesus replied, "Moses allowed you to divorce your wives because your hearts are unyielding. But it wasn't that way from the beginning. I say to you that whoever divorces his wife, except for sexual unfaithfulness, and marries another woman commits adultery" (Matthew 19:8-9). Once again,

Jesus did not take what was written in Scripture and say, "God said it, I believe it, that settles it." In this passage he makes clear that what was written in Scripture were Moses' words, not God's words.

Yet even on the subject of divorce, with Jesus' more conservative interpretation, look at his actions toward a woman who had been divorced five times, as described in John 4. In that case he demonstrated mercy and compassion, not judgment. Likewise his ministry with "sinners and tax collectors" reflected a more liberal approach to Scripture and its application than what was found among the Pharisees of his time.

So, even though Jesus affirmed the Law and the Prophets, he interpreted them sometimes more liberally, and other times more conservatively, than the Pharisees with whom he was regularly interacting.

Christians take Jesus' words about the Law and Prophets, quoted above from Matthew 5:17-20, and we interpret them. And it is not just modern interpreters who do this; Jesus' own apostles interpreted his words, taking them to mean that the Law was either (a) only binding upon Jews or (b) only binding until Jesus' death and resurrection fulfilled the old covenant and initiated a new covenant. We see the disciples wrestling with this question of the Law, and how to interpret Jesus' words concerning it, in a remarkable story recounted in Acts 15.

In Acts 15, Paul and Barnabas brought a question to the apostles and elders in Jerusalem. There were many non-Jews who had become followers of Jesus. Some Jewish Christians believed these non-Jews needed to be circumcised, for that was what the Scriptures commanded as a sign of God's covenant with Abraham and his descendants, a command reiterated in the Law of Moses. Ultimately the disciples of Jesus made the dramatic decision that neither circumcision nor most of the rest of the Law was binding upon non-Jewish followers of Jesus. What was most remarkable about the apostles' decision, from my perspective, was that it meant setting aside the binding nature of the Law, which was the most authoritative part of their Scriptures. (Jews at that time disagreed about the authority of various texts that constitute our Old Testament, but everyone agreed that the Law was authoritative.) In other words, the apostles were interpreting Jesus' words recorded in Matthew 5:17-20 in a certain way. The apostles didn't explain the entire theological rationale behind their decision, but what they clearly did not believe was that "God said it, I believe it, that settles it."

Here's the point I'm trying to make: Whether Christians admit it or not, we seldom actually read the Bible with the thought that God said it, I believe it, that settles it. I remember speaking to a Christian some years ago who said to me, "I don't interpret Scripture; I just take it all as God's Word and try to live it." I asked him, "So, you refrain from eating pork and you go to church on Saturday?" To which he replied, "Well, no, that's the Old Testament." "Okay, so you insist that your wife prays with her head covered, that your daughters not braid their hair, and that you have no savings accounts?" He replied, "No, those passages were about the times when the biblical authors lived, but not today." To which I replied, "In other words, you interpret Scripture!"

Whether Christians admit it or not, we seldom actually read the Bible with the thought that God said it, I believe it, that settles it.

The Bible on Women in the Church

We see this kind of Bible interpretation play out in a host of other ways. Several years ago, my wife, LaVon, and I went to a wedding like none we had ever attended. Instead of exchanging rings, the bride and groom exchanged Bibles. I realized that the couple was basing the ceremony on a very literal interpretation of 1 Timothy 2:9, which seems to prohibit jewelry: "I want women to enhance their appearance with clothing that is modest and sensible, not with elaborate hairstyles, gold, pearls, or expensive clothes." A very similar instruction is found in 1 Peter 3:3: "Don't try to make yourselves beautiful on the outside, with stylish hair or by wearing gold jewelry or fine clothes." How many Christians recite the mantra "God said it, I believe it, that settles it" yet wear expensive jewelry, braid their hair, and pray without their heads covered?

Other verses on women in the church are among the most interesting and seemingly anachronistic passages in the New Testament. A parenthetical comment from Paul in 1 Corinthians is a prime example:

As in all the churches of the saints, women should be silent in the churches. For they are not permitted to speak, but should be subordinate, as the law also says. If there is anything they desire to know, let them ask their husbands at home. For it is shameful for a woman to speak in church. (1 Corinthians 14:33b-35 NRSV)

More uncomfortable, perhaps, are the words that are attributed to Paul in 1 Timothy (just after the verse telling women not to wear gold or pearls or elaborate hairstyles):

Let a woman learn in silence with full submission. I permit no woman to teach or to have authority over a man; she is to keep silent.

(1 Timothy 2:11-12 NRSV)

Some churches continue to read these verses as though they reflect God's will for all time. In these churches, women are not allowed to serve in leadership, to teach Bible studies or Sunday school classes where men are present, or to serve in any capacity during worship that would require them to speak to the congregation. But even most of these churches do not require women to pray with their heads covered, despite the fact that Paul writes:

> Every woman who prays or prophesies with her
> head uncovered disgraces her head. It is the same
> thing as having her head shaved. If a woman
> doesn't cover her head, then she should have her
> hair cut off. (1 Corinthians 11:5-6a)

When reading these words, few would respond,
"God said it, I believe it, that settles it."

The Bible on Human Slavery

An extremely literal approach to the Bible was
used frequently in the 1840s, 1850s, and 1860s by
preachers who argued that slavery was part of God's
social order. They pointed to more than two hundred
verses in the Bible that address slavery and regulate
its practice, saying that the prevalence of such verses
seemed to indicate that the practice was acceptable
to God. This conclusion is particularly surprising,
given that God delivered the Israelites from slavery
in Egypt. How do we reconcile these two seemingly
contradictory actions by God?

Some, in trying to address this thorny question, note
that slavery in biblical times was far different from
slavery as practiced in the United States. It's true there
undoubtedly were differences in how one became

a slave, but the basic act of owning another human being, including the ability of masters to discipline their slaves with beatings, was common to both biblical and modern slavery. Exodus 21:20-21 captures both ideas when Moses gives this command: "When a slave owner hits a male or female slave with a rod and the slave dies immediately, the owner should be punished. But if the slave gets up after a day or two, the slave owner shouldn't be punished *because the slave is the owner's property.*"

Because the Scriptures speak of slavery so often, advocates of slavery in the United States argued that the institution was acceptable to God. As the historian John Patrick Daly wrote, "Moral and biblical justification of slaveholding constituted the first, and remained the most widely disseminated, foundation of southern proslavery."[4] He notes, "It would be hard to exaggerate the importance of ethical and exegetical arguments" in solidifying southern support of slavery.

Many a slave owner could quote Luke 12:47 by heart. The verse reads: "That slave who knew what his master wanted, but did not prepare himself or do what was wanted, will receive a severe beating" (NRSV). If you saw the film *Twelve Years a Slave*, you heard a harsh slave master recite a version of this verse,

Bible in hand. He cited it to justify beatings the slaves received from him and the overseers who worked for him. However, in the passage Jesus was using slaves to illustrate a point, not to endorse slavery. With passages concerning slavery, the slave owners seemed to act out of a view of Scripture that holds, "God said it, I believe it, that settles it." Tragically, they missed many other passages about justice, mercy, and love.

The Problem with "God Said It"

"God said it, I believe it, that settles it" may not be as helpful as we think when it comes to interpreting the Bible, nor does it reflect the way Jesus and the apostles looked at Scripture. Part of the reason is that it tends to oversimplify what Scripture is and how we are to read it. It assumes that the words of Scripture were, in essence, dictated by God to the biblical authors.

Is it really true that "God said it"? There are indeed passages in which the biblical authors claim they literally received God's words. For example, Moses at times says that God dictated sections of the Law; the prophets sometimes say (as in Jeremiah 1:4), "The LORD's word came to me . . ."; the writer of Revelation claims at points that the Lord spoke directly to him and commanded him to write down certain things (though often it is an angel or merely a voice that he claims is speaking to him in a vision). Yet most of the time, the biblical authors do not claim any form of dictation but claim to be writing their own insights, reflections, and ideas concerning God's will.

Most of the time, the biblical authors claim to be writing their own insights, reflections, and ideas concerning God's will.

In Paul's letters, he never claims that his words and thoughts are synonymous with God's words and thoughts. He does, however, trust that he is led by the Spirit. In response to questions from believers in his churches, he writes to teach, encourage, correct, and mentor his flock. Does God speak through him in this? Of course. Does God still speak through Paul's words to us today? Absolutely. But since he is writing as Paul and not God, we must interpret his words. We must seek to understand the times in which Paul wrote, the circumstances he was addressing, and the ways in which his words continue to address our current situation. When Paul corresponded with churches and individuals, do you think he expected them to say of his letters, "God said it, I believe it, that settles it"? I seriously doubt it. I do believe he counted on people to take his letters seriously because he was an apostle, was led by the Spirit, and had devoted years to studying the Scriptures and reflecting upon, preaching, and living the gospel.

When people speak about Scripture, they often refer to its inspiration. Interestingly, the word *inspired* with reference to Scripture appears only once in the Bible, and this is found in 2 Timothy 3:16-17, where we read,

> Every scripture is inspired by God and is useful for teaching, for showing mistakes, for correcting, and for training character, so that the person who belongs to God can be equipped to do everything that is good.

We tend to bring our own assumptions to the task of interpreting this verse. A few things should be noted.

First, when Paul uses the word *scripture*, he is referring to the documents that make up our Old Testament. (The Gospels, Acts, Revelation, and most general epistles in the New Testament were not written by the time of Paul's death, and it is unlikely he was referring to his own letters as scripture.) And when Paul writes that "every scripture" is inspired by God, he likely is *not* referring to every word or verse in the Old Testament, but instead is addressing a question of which individual writings circulating among Jewish communities in the first century as holy books were influenced by God.*

But it may be that Paul's use of "every scripture" was in response to a different debate. In Paul's day, Sadducees and Samaritans considered only the Torah (the Law) to be authoritative and did not give the same weight to the Prophets or to other Writings that we consider part of the Old Testament. Paul was a Pharisee, and the Pharisees did count the Prophets and Writings as authoritative. When Paul wrote that "every scripture is inspired by God," he may have been saying that the Torah, the Prophets, and the Writings are all inspired by God (as against the

---

* Jews in Alexandria, Egypt, from whom the Greek version of the Old Testament writings came, included in their scriptures a handful of texts that the Jews in Jerusalem did not count as authoritative. (Most of these texts, known as the *deuterocanonical books*, are included in the Roman Catholic and Orthodox versions of the Old Testament.) It is possible that by using the phrase "every scripture," Paul was affirming the texts counted sacred in the Greek Old Testament canon—that is, the library of Old Testament texts used in the Greek-speaking world where Paul devoted most of his time.

Sadducees who claimed only the Torah carried this kind of authority).

In interpreting 2 Timothy 3:16, it is also important to ask what Paul meant when he said that every scripture is "inspired by God." In Greek this phrase is just one word, *theopneustos*. It appears nowhere else in the Bible, nor as far as we know in other ancient literature, prior to Paul's use of the word here. It comes from two words: *theo*, which means God, and *pneustos*, which refers to breath, wind, or spirit. What specifically does Paul mean by this word? Once more we must interpret, for Paul does not explain. We can say for certain Paul believed that in some sense all the sacred writings were influenced by God. Precisely how, we can only speculate.

In this passage of the letter to Timothy, Paul is not trying to teach a doctrine of inspiration ("God said it") but to make clear that God's influence on the Jewish sacred writings makes them "useful for teaching, for showing mistakes, for correcting, and for training character, so that the person who belongs to God can be equipped to do everything that is good."

This is in fact how Scripture functions for us: it helps form and shape our understanding of who God is and what God's will is for our lives, so that we can be equipped to do what is good.

The Bible contains the defining story of my life. Its words and teachings shape who I am and who I hope to be. I study it daily, praying that God will speak to me as I do. But I read it recognizing that the biblical authors were people, writing for various purposes and for specific audiences in particular historical circumstances. These authors related their experiences of God—the way they heard him speak, as well as the things they thought and believed about God and God's will for their lives. God was at work in them, influencing their writing, and God continues to influence all of us as we read their words. That is far different from saying, "God said it, I believe it, that settles it."*

---

* Not to beat a dead horse, but it is of some value to reiterate that the Law was at the center and foundation of the Jewish Scriptures Paul was referring to in 2 Timothy 3:16, and the Law was inspired by God. Yet whatever the phrase "inspired by God" meant to Paul, it still allowed him to say that believers are no longer "under Law but under grace" (Romans 6:14-15) and that "we have been released from the Law" (Romans 7:6). Paul might summarize this point regarding the Law and its primary requirement in this way: "Whoever loves another person has fulfilled the Law" (Romans 13:8).

The Problem with "That Settles It"

We've seen that "God said it" is an overly simplistic way of understanding God's involvement with Scripture. Unlike Muslims, who believe God dictated (through the angel Gabriel) the words of the Qur'an to Muhammad, Christians do not believe this is the way we received our Scriptures.

"That settles it" is also overly simplistic. The fact is, when we see something written in Scripture, that doesn't settle it. A whole host of factors go into understanding the biblical text.

First, scholars help determine the most likely reading of the text in its original language. We don't have the original manuscripts of the biblical texts. What we do have is an amazing trove of ancient manuscripts that are copies of the biblical texts, and they are generally very close to one another in what they say. But in places there are differences in wording—variants—and scholars must decide which variant is most likely what the biblical author wrote. This is a science known as textual criticism, and scholars acknowledge that, while the text we have now is pretty good, the choices are not completely settled, and new discoveries of ancient texts might change their conclusions.

Next comes the work of translating the original Hebrew, Aramaic, and Greek texts into English. (The Old Testament is written primarily in Hebrew, with a small number of passages in Aramaic, while the New Testament was written entirely in Greek.) The translation task is itself a work of interpretation. Most Hebrew, Aramaic, and Greek words, like English words, can have different meanings depending upon the context. Consider the well-loved John 3:16. The best-known version is the King James: "For God so loved the world, that he gave his only begotten Son, that whosoever believeth in him should not perish, but have everlasting life." The word *perish* in Greek is *apollumi* which can mean perish, but also simply to die, to be destroyed, to be lost, killed, or ruined. Each of these different words might change the verse's meaning slightly. Translators at times disagree on what word best communicates the intent of the original author; hence, different translations offer different readings and at times different meanings. This is why I use a number of different translations when preparing sermons, and why at times I go back to the original languages. The debates among Bible translators remind us that the English text of the Bible is not completely settled.

But once we start reading the text, as described above, we immediately begin interpreting it. The technical terms for this work are *hermeneutics* and *exegesis*. The task involves seeking to understand the passage's historical context, what precipitated its writing, what it meant to the original audience, and then the way or ways in which it might speak to people today.

This work of understanding the intended meaning of a text and expounding on its contemporary meaning was never settled in ancient Judaism (nor in modern Judaism). Jews debated the meaning of Scripture and its application in what became a vast oral commentary including the debate among great rabbis on how to interpret various texts, stories related to the texts, and applications. This oral commentary began to be written down in the second century after Christ. The word *Midrash* is used to describe the process of debating various texts and expounding on their meaning, as well as to describe the actual written commentaries on the Jewish scriptures. The *Mishnah* is the Oral Law of the Jews—that is, their attempts to apply, interpret, and expound upon the Law of Moses. This Oral Law was written down in the second century. In addition to the Midrash and Mishnah, Jews also have the *Talmud*, a vast written body of the teaching and reflections of great rabbis who sought to explain the Mishnah and the Scriptures and apply them to daily life. The great rabbis who were involved in study, debate, and application of the Scriptures would have found it odd to say, "God says it, I believe it, that settles it."

Keep in mind that Jesus was a part of this rabbinical tradition. He was often pushing back against prevailing interpretations of Scripture among the rabbis of his day. You can hear this in the Sermon on the Mount when Jesus repeatedly says, "You have heard that it was said..." and then quotes a Scripture or a part of the Oral Law followed by the words "But I say to you..." and then offers a different interpretation of the text from the prevailing one.

Jesus was often pushing back against prevailing interpretations of Scripture among the rabbis of his day.

In many ways, the apostles in their New Testament writings are doing midrash—that is, they are reinterpreting the Scriptures of the Hebrew Bible and, as we've seen above in Paul's letters, even reinterpreting the very purpose of the Law itself.

Paul and the apostles took the Bible seriously. They believed God spoke through Scripture, but they also vigorously debated its meaning and at times offered very different interpretations from those held by other Jews of the time. The apostles understood that the various biblical authors were people, writing under the influence of God but also bringing their own circumstances and reflections to bear as they wrote. This is why the apostles could debate the meaning of Scripture. It's why they would not have stated, "God said it, I believe it, that settles it."

Like the apostles, we read Scripture and hear God speak through it. But we also ask questions of it. We consider context. We interpret. We wonder if God really intended women to remain silent in the church. We recognize that slavery cannot be God's will, despite more than two hundred verses in the Bible that support it. We don't preach that having bathrooms inside our houses of worship is offensive to God.

The Definitive Word of God

So, how do we make sense of Scripture today? How do we apply it to our lives? How do we decide that something should be taken figuratively rather than literally or that a particular verse may not apply to us at all anymore? Thankfully, it may not be as complicated as the above discussion has implied.

We have access to great commentaries and study Bibles that can help. Our pastors and churches are meant to guide us—in sermons, in Bible studies, in one-on-one conversations over a cup of coffee. Friends doing Bible study can consider together the meaning of a text and how it applies to us in the modern world. These are some of the ways in which Christians today do the same kind of midrashic work that our Jewish friends have been doing for more than three thousand years (and which most Christians have been doing for two thousand years).

It's important to recognize that when we study Scripture, our own biases can lead us to hear what we want to hear. Conservatives, seeing Jesus as a conservative, tend to find Scripture passages that line up with their own viewpoints and gloss over passages that do not. Progressives do the same. Like the slave owners and their preachers in the mid-nineteenth century, we focus on certain passages and ignore others in seeking support for our views. Small groups that have little information about the Bible might have lengthy discussions on a particular text but end up far afield of the likely meaning, as the discussion devolves into a case of the proverbial "blind leading the blind."

But if we try to set aside our biases, using some basic tools and bringing our intellect and experience to bear, we'll find Bible study to be a great adventure. We'll discover new truths in the text. We'll see things— even though we've read the verse dozens of times— that we've never seen before. That's the blessing we receive in realizing that the meaning of the text is not completely settled and that God continues to speak through the Bible in new and fresh ways.

For me, the most important lens for interpreting Scripture is Jesus himself and his words. When a Scripture text seems inconsistent with something Jesus says or the way he acts, and I have to choose between the two, I'll choose Jesus every time. John describes Jesus as God's Word that became flesh: he is the definitive Word of God. All other words in

Scripture were mediated through ordinary human beings, many of whose names we know—Moses, David, John, Paul. But Christians believe that in Jesus, God came to us, walked among us, showed us, and taught us who God is and who we are meant to be.

One of the things Jesus said that I think is of utmost importance in reading and interpreting Scripture occurred when he was asked which commandment is the greatest. Jesus answered,

> "'You shall love the Lord your God with all your heart, and with all your soul, and with all your mind.' This is the greatest and first commandment. And a second is like it: 'You shall love your neighbor as yourself.' On these two commandments hang all the law and the prophets." (Matthew 22:37-40 NRSV)

The first commandment was assumed by most of the New Testament authors. But the second was explicitly repeated again and again in the New Testament Epistles. Nearly all the New Testament authors repeat the command to love.

When we seek to read and understand Scripture, Christians should interpret it through the lens of what Jesus teaches us about the heart, character, and will of God, and through the commands to love God and others. In this regard, a friend of mine compared Jesus and the great commandments to the use of a colander. A colander is a strainer used to wash vegetables, so you can rinse off dirt and other things you don't want to eat, leaving just the food. My friend noted that when reading Scripture, we should question passages that are inconsistent with the things Jesus said or did, or with the commands to love God and neighbor.

When we seek to read and understand Scripture, Christians should interpret it through the lens of what Jesus teaches us about the heart, character, and will of God, and through the commands to love God and others.

As an example, we read in Leviticus 20:10 that the penalty for adultery was death. But a woman caught in the act of adultery was brought to Jesus by a crowd about to stone her. (Might they have believed, "God said it, I believe it, that settles it"?) Seeing the woman, Jesus told them, "Whoever hasn't sinned should throw the first stone" (John 8:7b). The people dropped their stones, one by one, and walked away. Jesus did not excuse her adultery; he forgave it and commanded her not to sin again. When our colander is Jesus, capital punishment for adultery falls through and is washed away.

I was speaking at a conference on this very topic, using the colander metaphor, when a young pastor said it sounded like I was "picking and choosing," a phrase often used to criticize those who advocate for properly interpreting Scripture, implying that the one criticizing does not "pick and choose." I asked him whether he was participating in our denomination's pension fund, in which he and his church contributed funds for his retirement. He replied that he was participating. I asked him, "What part of Jesus' command not to store up treasures on earth did you not understand?" I asked the question lightheartedly but wanted to point out that we might all be accused of picking and choosing at times. Properly interpreting the Scriptures and seeking to apply them to our daily lives is not "picking and choosing."

In the case of Jesus' command not to store up treasures on earth, we recognize that he lived in a time when social security meant multiple generations of families living under one roof, with the younger generations caring for their elders. But today we don't often do that, and so saving for retirement becomes a way of helping our children and others. Likewise, having emergency funds in savings is better than going into debt when faced with a surprise medical bill or home repair. So we read Jesus' words today and rather than taking them literally, consider seriously the point behind them: Don't make the acquisition and saving of money your focus in life. Don't let money and possessions become your *de facto* god. None of these things will last.

A few years ago, A. J. Jacobs wrote a book titled *The Year of Living Biblically*, in which for one year he tried to practice literally everything commanded in the Law. It became clear to him that it was impossible to literally practice everything commanded in Scripture. Among his conclusions at the end of the year was that everyone picks and chooses. What's important is to pick the right things.

I love the Bible. I read from it every morning. I've memorized many of its passages. Each week I seek not only to preach its words for my congregation but also to live them. Reading the Bible as a fourteen-year-old boy changed my life, and as a fifty-one-year-old man my life continues to be changed by reading it. Yet there are many times when I wrestle with how to make sense of it.

It's a half truth to say, "God said it, I believe it, that settles it." My version of that statement might not fit on a bumper sticker, but I believe it's more truthful: "God influenced it. I read, study, and sometimes wrestle with it. And, as I interpret it in the light of Jesus Christ, I hear God speak through it and seek to live its words as best I can."

Dear God, how grateful we are for your love and grace. How grateful we are that you gave us the Scriptures as a gift, for us to know you and know your purposes and will. How grateful we are that you sent Jesus Christ to be the Word made flesh. Help us to understand the Scriptures. O God, when we look at Jesus, we see you. Help us to be people after his own heart. Help us to be people who read the Scriptures, study them, memorize them, and seek to live them as they align with the person and the teachings of Jesus. Amen.

5.

LOVE THE SINNER,
HATE THE SIN

[Jesus said to them,] "Don't judge, so that you won't be judged. You'll receive the same judgment you give. Whatever you deal out will be dealt out to you. Why do you see the splinter that's in your brother's or sister's eye, but don't notice the log in your own eye? How can you say to your brother or sister, 'Let me take the splinter out of your eye,' when there's a log in your eye? You deceive yourself! First take the log out of your eye, and then you'll see clearly to take the splinter out of your brother's or sister's eye."

—Matthew 7:1-5

5.

Love the Sinner, Hate the Sin

The final half truth we'll deal with may be the one I see and hear most often these days. Like the other clichés, it sounds so right that it's hard to imagine what could possibly be wrong with it. And, like the others, you will often hear it from Christians with good intentions. Many who say it mean it to be gracious and kind, and it reflects their love of people. One woman I recently saw felt so strongly about this expression that she had it tattooed to her arm: Love the sinner, hate the sin.

Another half truth is often quoted in the same breath with this one: "No sin is worse than any other."

These words, too, are spoken with good intentions. The speakers usually mean that they are not being judgmental when they point out sin, as in: "I'm a sinner too. We are all sinners, and no sin is worse than any other. I'm not condemning you—who am I to condemn, since my sins are as bad as yours?"

As with some of the other half truths we have examined in this book, a number of Christians believe that the statement "Love the sinner, hate the sin" is found in Scripture, and perhaps is even a statement of Jesus himself. But Jesus never said this, nor does the sentiment behind it reflect the kinds of things he said. Rather, the phrase seems to have originated with St. Augustine, a bishop from North Africa who lived in the late fourth and early fifth centuries. In his capacity as a church leader, Augustine was writing a letter to nuns, asking them to remain chaste. In the letter he called them to have a "love for mankind and hatred of sins." However, it's doubtful that Augustine meant to coin a phrase that Christians would use to describe their dislike of someone else's sins.

Mahatma Gandhi wrote something similar in his 1929 autobiography, but he added an important thought. Most readers stop at his quote, "Hate the sin and not the sinner," but the full statement reads: "Hate the sin and not the sinner is a precept which, though easy enough to understand, is rarely practiced, and that is why the poison of hatred spreads in the world." Gandhi was not advocating the idea of this half truth; I believe he was observing that most find it hard to hate another's sin without harming the sinner.

What Is Sin?

Let's begin with the definition of sin. In the Old Testament, a variety of words are translated as the English word *sin*, most frequent among them the Hebrew verb *chata*. In the New Testament, the most commonly used word for sin is the Greek word *hamartia*. Both of these words essentially mean "to stray from the path" or "to miss the mark," where the path or mark is God's intention or will for us. So, sin can apply to any thought, word, or action that is contrary to God's will. It can even apply to a failure to act or to do something we should do, as when we see someone who is hurting or in need and don't stop to help. By not helping we have sinned. We have deviated from the path that God calls us to follow.

We all sin. None of us lives a perfect life. We think, say, and do things we should not, and we fail to think, say, and do things we should. In his Letter to the Romans, Paul states it this way: "All have sinned and fall short of God's glory" (Romans 3:23). Later in that letter he speaks of the struggles we face in doing the right things and refraining from doing the wrong things: "I don't do the good that I want to do, but I do the evil that I don't want to do" (Romans 7:19).

We all sin. None of us lives a perfect life. We think, say, and do things we should not, and we fail to think, say, and do things we should.

If all of us sin, then is it true, as some Christians say, that all sins are equal? If we study the Bible and apply common sense, the answer is clear: No, not all sins are equal.

Eating a dozen Krispy Kreme donuts in one sitting is an act of gluttony, and gluttony is not God's will. If this practice becomes a regular part of our eating pattern, it's not healthy and can cut our lives short. But is eating a dozen donuts equal in God's eyes to driving while intoxicated with the potential of killing another human being? Both are sins, but one has the potential to kill or seriously maim others. These are both sins that start with overconsuming, but the potential consequences are very, very different.

Or consider swearing. Is swearing on the golf course equal to swearing in a court of law that someone has committed a crime he or she did not commit? Is cheating in a card game of the same magnitude in God's eyes as cheating on your spouse? No, not all sins are equal.

What does the Bible say? We may get confused when we read Jesus' comments about sin that he made in the Sermon on the Mount. In this sermon, as mentioned previously, Jesus contrasted prevailing views of Scripture with his own views. At one point he says, "You have heard that it was said to those who lived long ago, *Don't commit murder*, and all who commit murder will be in danger of judgment. But I say to you that everyone who is angry with their brother or sister will be in danger of judgment" (Matthew 5:21-22a). Elsewhere he says, "You have heard that it was said, *Don't commit adultery*. But I say to you that every man who looks at a woman lustfully has already committed adultery in his heart" (vv. 27-28).

If contemplating a sin is the same as actually committing that sin, then of course it's easy to conclude that all sins are equal. But that's not exactly what Jesus is saying. Instead, engaging in what some call "prophetic hyperbole," he speaks in a prophetic voice that calls us to examine carefully our thoughts and actions, and he exaggerates to make a point.

In the next verse of the Sermon on the Mount, Jesus continues his use of prophetic hyperbole by saying, "If your right eye causes you to fall into sin, tear it out and throw it away. It's better that you lose a part of your body than that your whole body be thrown into hell. And if your right hand causes you to fall into sin, chop it off and throw it away. It's better that you lose a part of your body than that your whole body go into hell" (Matthew 5:29-30). Is Jesus really suggesting we pluck out our eyes and cut off our hands? Or is he saying, "Sin is serious business, and do everything you can to avoid it"?

Roman Catholics have two specific terms to describe the varying seriousness and severity of sins. *Venial sins* are those that are less serious and more readily forgiven; these may also occur without a person's full knowledge or engagement of the will.

Mortal sins, on the other hand, are grave violations of God's will. These are committed knowingly and willingly, and they have the potential to cause significant harm to ourselves, to others, and to our relationship with God.

Catholic teaching draws the idea of differing degrees of sin from 1 John 5:16-17:

> "If anyone sees a brother or sister committing a sin *that does not result in death*, they should pray, and God will give life to them—that is, to those who commit sins that don't result in death. *There is a sin that results in death*—I'm not saying that you should pray about that. Every unrighteous action is sin, but there is a sin that does not result in death." [Emphasis added]

Even if you can't recite the Seven Deadly Sins from memory, you're likely familiar with them. Sometimes these are also called the "capital sins," because Roman Catholic teaching holds that all other sins emerge from these seven. In traditional order, the sins are:

1. lust
2. gluttony
3. greed
4. sloth
5. wrath
6. envy
7. pride

Even among these "root" sins, not all offenses are created equal. The Catholic Church considers one of them to be deadlier and more dangerous than the others. It isn't lust, greed, or even wrath. It's pride. Why? Because, in the church's understanding, all the other sins arise from pride.

The idea that all sins are equal is an underpinning for the half truth of "Love the sinner, hate the sin." Like the half truth itself, this Christian cliché about all sin being equal not only lacks a solid scriptural foundation, but upon further examination is shown to be counter to what is taught in Scripture.

Having spent a few minutes examining and weighing sin, let's take a closer look at the half truth "Love the sinner, hate the sin." My hope is that, when we're finished, you might scrub this statement from your spiritual vocabulary.

Love the Sinner

Let's begin by recognizing that the first part of this half truth is actually true. Of course we are called to love sinners! It's a message we encounter in the New

Testament over and over again. Jesus did it all the time. It was a critical part of his life and ministry. He was called a friend of sinners. Paul writes in 1 Timothy 1:15, "This saying is reliable and deserves full acceptance: 'Christ Jesus came into the world to save sinners.'" Then Paul adds: "And I'm the biggest sinner of all." If Jesus didn't love sinners, he didn't love *us*.

Though Jesus certainly loved sinners, he never actually said, "Love the sinner." What he did say (and it's an important distinction) is "Love your neighbor."

The problem—and the danger for us—is that the statement "Love the sinner," while true as far as it goes, is not what Jesus commanded us to do, and it can actually lead us to sin by violating something Jesus did teach his disciples. Though Jesus certainly loved sinners, he never actually said, "Love the sinner." What he did say (and it's an important distinction) is "Love your neighbor."

As Jesus' teaching made clear, your neighbor is everyone you meet, and even those you haven't met. Your neighbor includes anyone who needs your help. When people donate goods to the Super Bowl Food Drive at our congregation, they are showing love to neighbors they probably never will meet. When our offerings help people who have been affected by natural disasters, in another state or even another continent, we are answering the call to love our neighbors—fellow human beings made in the image of God who, like us, are children of God. To love them as neighbors does not mean we necessarily have warm feelings for them. It doesn't even mean that we have to like them personally. It means doing good to them, seeking to bless and encourage them. It means showing kindness to them, though they have no right to claim this from us.

Jesus, of course, goes even further in explaining who our neighbors are. He expressly commands us to love our enemies—people who have wronged us, people who might not do unto us as they wish others would do toward them. As with all our neighbors, we are to seek good for our enemies. In fact, we are to love our enemies especially, because Jesus teaches that when we do, the world changes. Jesus tells us not to return evil for evil or take an eye for an eye. (As Gandhi is said to have observed, "An eye for an eye makes the whole world blind.") Instead, when we show love to our enemies, when we return blessings for evil, we create possibilities for transformed situations and relationships.

So, if we are called to love our neighbors and love our enemies, why doesn't Jesus ever say, "Love the sinner"?

First, and most basically, such a command would be redundant, since the neighbor and the enemy are both sinners. Every sinner is my neighbor, and some also are my enemy. Since all of us are sinners, telling us to love our neighbors already covers everyone!

More importantly, I think Jesus knew that if he commanded his disciples to "love the sinner," they would begin looking at other people more as sinners than as neighbors. And that, inevitably, would lead to judgment. If I love you more as a sinner than as my neighbor, then I am bound to focus more on your sin. I will start looking for all the things that are wrong with you. And perhaps, without intending it, I will begin thinking of our relationship like this: "You are a sinner, but I graciously choose to love you any-way." If that sounds a little puffed up, self-righteous, and even prideful to you, then you have perceived accurately.

I think Jesus well understood the human tendency to judge others and focus on their sin—and this is why, in the Gospels, Jesus taught that we should avoid it. Instead, we should focus simply on loving our neighbors, including our neighbors who are enemies.

For example, Jesus told a parable about a Pharisee and a tax collector. The Pharisees were religious leaders who believed they needed to separate them-selves from sinners in order to remain pure and holy to God. (In Hebrew, the word *pharisee* likely meant "set apart" or "the separated ones.") By contrast, tax collectors in Jesus' day were commonly considered the worst kind of sinners, in that they collaborated with the Roman occupying force, making them traitors to their own people. Here's the story Jesus told about these two figures:

> "Two people went up to the temple to pray. One was a Pharisee and the other a tax collector. The Pharisee stood and prayed about himself with

these words, 'God, I thank you that I'm not like everyone else—crooks, evildoers, adulterers—or even like this tax collector. I fast twice a week. I give a tenth of everything I receive.' But the tax collector stood at a distance. He wouldn't even lift his eyes to look toward heaven. Rather, he struck his chest and said, 'God, show mercy to me, a sinner.' I tell you, this person went down to his home justified rather than the Pharisee. All who lift themselves up will be brought low, and those who make themselves low will be lifted up." (Luke 18:10-14)

When "Love the sinner" is our mantra, we've put ourselves in a position of seeing others as sinners rather than neighbors, and though we may emphasize that we also are sinners (some of the Pharisee seemed to miss this part), our focus on the other as sinner rather than as neighbor defines our relationship: "I will love you despite the fact that you are a sinner."

> **When "Love the sinner" is our mantra, we've put ourselves in a position of seeing others as sinners rather than neighbors.**

Luke introduces the parable of the Pharisee and tax collector with these words: "Jesus told this parable to certain people who had convinced themselves that they were righteous and who looked on everyone else with disgust" (v. 9). Have you ever met people like that? Were they pleasant to be around? Perhaps more importantly, are you ever like that?

Take another look at the Scripture passage at the beginning of this chapter, found near the end of Jesus' Sermon on the Mount. In it, Jesus is speaking not only to the multitudes present that day, but more importantly to his own disciples.

> "Don't judge, so that you won't be judged. You'll receive the same judgment you give. Whatever you deal out will be dealt out to you. Why do you see the splinter that's in your brother's or sister's eye, but don't notice the log in your own eye? How can you say to your brother or sister, 'Let me take the splinter out of your eye,' when there's a log in your eye? You deceive yourself! First take the log out of your eye, and then you'll see clearly to take the splinter out of your brother's or sister's eye." (Matthew 7:1-5)

Jesus knew that the disciples themselves would struggle with the tendency to judge others. It was this judgmentalism that Jesus wanted his disciples (then and now) to avoid. After all, Jesus' nonjudgmental approach was part of what drew people to him, just as the judgmental approach of some Pharisees repelled many sinners. As he did so often, Jesus used a graphic, memorable metaphor: the splinter in your brother's or sister's eye, compared with the log in your own eye.

Jesus' listeners could immediately grasp the absurdity of what he was describing. They may have chuckled, as my congregation did the last time I preached on this parable, when I held a log to my right eye while grasping a pair of tweezers as if to remove the splinter from their eyes. The point, though, was a serious one. Jesus was saying that judging others is not something his disciples should do.

If Jesus wouldn't say "Love the sinner," what would he say instead? I think it might be something like this: "Love your neighbor despite the fact that *you* are a sinner." In other words, as a follower of Jesus I will love you because you're a person who needs love. And though I'm a sinner, you deserve my love because God first loved me. I will love you because Jesus said love is the way his disciples are meant to live. I will love you because I believe that love has the power to change the world.

Hate the Sin

As we've seen, "Love the sinner" presents difficulties. However, the second part of this half truth—"Hate the sin"—is where the real problem arises.

As the Gospels make a point of showing us, Jesus spent time with drunkards, prostitutes, thieves, the occasional adulterer, traitors to their own people, and countless others who undoubtedly had impure thoughts, cheated on their taxes, and committed a variety of crimes. He routinely broke bread with them, healed them, and even called them to be his disciples. Yet we never hear Jesus say to them, "I love you, but I hate your sin."

When Jesus speaks to sinful people, he doesn't talk about their sin but about God's forgiveness. In Luke 7, a woman who may be a prostitute crashes a dinner party at the home of a man named Simon. Jesus is the guest of honor. When the woman enters, the host is aghast. The woman weeps before Jesus, then anoints his feet with oil and dries them with her hair. Simon wonders why Jesus would allow such a woman to touch him. Jesus gently rebukes Simon, then says to the woman, "Your sins are forgiven."

When Jesus speaks to sinful people, he doesn't talk about their sin but about God's forgiveness.

As the Gospels relate it, the only time when Jesus seems to demonstrate a hatred of sin occurs when the sin is committed by religious leaders. For example, Jesus is so angered by the sight of merchants in the temple ripping off the poor—charging them exorbitant rates to exchange their currency or to buy animals as sacrifices to God—that he overturns the money changers' tables. He is especially disdainful toward the religious leaders' hypocrisy, declaring in Matthew what are commonly called the "seven woes." Here is one of them:

> "How terrible it will be for you legal experts and Pharisees! Hypocrites! You are like whitewashed tombs. They look beautiful on the outside. But inside they are full of dead bones and all kinds of filth. In the same way you look righteous to people. But inside you are full of pretense and rebellion." (Matthew 23:27-28)

You've no doubt heard people describe why they don't go to church. Among the top answers: religious hypocrisy. In my experience, these people understand that we're all hypocrites and that no one perfectly lives out what they believe. I think what turns people off is when religious people point out the sins of others but act as though they have no sins of their own.

Somebody recently gave me a cartoon depicting St. Peter standing at the pearly gates. A person who has just died stands in front of Peter, hoping for admission into heaven. As Peter finds the appropriate page in the Book of Life, he says, "You were a believer, yes, but you skipped the 'not being a jerk about it' part.'"

My hope is to be a Christian without being a jerk. I'd like to help the people in my congregation to be Christians without being jerks. And I'd like to encourage you who are reading this book to be Christians without being jerks.

To support the idea of loving the sinner and hating the sin, some people point to Romans 12:9, where Paul writes, "Love should be shown without pretending. Hate evil, and hold on to what is good." But notice that Paul is not telling his readers to hate the sin in someone else's life; he's telling them to hate the evil *they* might be tempted to pursue in their own lives. Don't pretend to show love, then judge in the very next breath. Instead, "Let love be genuine" (NRSV).

Some time ago I read an interview with Billy Graham's eldest daughter, Gigi. She was her father's date to *Time* magazine's seventy-fifth anniversary party, a banquet in Washington, DC. President Bill Clinton spoke at the event. He had just been impeached by the House of Representatives for perjury and obstruction of justice. The charge of perjury involved what President Clinton had said, under oath, about his relationship with White House intern Monica Lewinsky.

At the banquet, her father sat with President and Mrs. Clinton. He was warm and gracious to them. After the dinner ended and Graham and Gigi were riding back to their hotel, the two discussed difficulties the president and First Lady were going through with so many people gossiping and judging. Gigi said her father's simple comment was, "It's the Holy Spirit's job to convict; it's God's job to judge; and it's our job to love."[5]

Christ's Call to Love

Should we keep silent about the problem of sin? Of course not. There are sins we must hate and denounce: sins that harm, oppress, or do evil to others, such as child abuse, spousal abuse, racism, injustice, and indifference to others. We should hate that children routinely die of starvation in our world of plenty. We should hate that people are victims of human trafficking. There is an appropriate righteous indignation over sins such as these, because part of our witness as Christians is to stand up to evil and resist it. Generally, though, when we use the phrase "Love the sinner, hate the sin," that's not what we're talking about.

In fact, these days when I hear "Love the sinner, hate the sin," it most often is part of a discussion about homosexuality. As a society we're divided about the question of same-sex marriage, just as Christians are in the church. Our Scriptures contain a handful of passages from Moses and Paul that clearly disapprove of some forms of same-sex practice that were observed in the times when these men lived.

An increasing number of Christians, including myself, question whether these verses in Moses and Paul convey God's will for his gay and lesbian children. Is it possible that the verses are addressing certain same-sex acts that even gay and lesbian people would condemn today? Some ask if the biblical authors conceived of the concept of sexual orientation as we understand it today. Still others suggest that the verses that speak of same-sex acts may be similar to the many verses that permit and regulate slavery, or those New Testament verses that insist that women not speak or teach in church—verses most of us today recognize reflect the cultural norms of the time more than the will of God. I discuss this topic in more detail elsewhere.* My own conclusions, after studying the Scriptures and the issue of homosexuality and ministering with people for the last thirty years, mirror these above. But I have many friends and church members who hold a more conservative view on this issue.

But what we agree upon, I hope, is the clarity around Christ's call to love one another. Love is what Jesus repeatedly demonstrated to sinners. It's what Billy Graham modeled for his daughter and the Clinton family. Our job is not to convict but to love.

Our job is not to convict but to love.

One Sunday, a gay couple who had been visiting our church came up and spoke to me after worship. They said, "We were sitting in the sanctuary, and at

---

* I've sought to capture my own understanding of these questions, particularly as they relate to the biblical text, in my book *Making Sense of the Bible* (New York: HarperOne, 2014).

one point we were holding hands. One of your older members leaned forward and handed us a note. We thought you'd want to see it."

My mind raced as I imagined what might be on that note. Mentally I groaned, fearing the note had been hurtful to the couple. When I opened it, here's what I saw: "I just want you to know how glad I am that you are in worship with us today. You are welcome in this church." The woman who wrote that note signed her first name. She is one of our senior adults and a pillar in the church. I never knew her position on same-sex relationships, but I've always known that she sought to make love the defining quality of her life.

Yes, there is sin in the world. When that sin is inflicted upon others, bringing harm to them, we must, in the words of the Proverbs, "Speak out on behalf of the voiceless, and for the rights of all who are vulnerable" (Proverbs 31:8). We're to be painfully aware of our own sin and regularly invite God to transform us, heal us, and forgive us. We're also to recognize that we may not see clearly how God sees, nor understand fully how God understands. What we can see clearly, and what is unmistakable regarding God's will, is that we love.

The truth in "Love the sinner, hate the sin" stops with the first word: *Love*. Let's love one another and strive to lay aside our own sin, while demonstrating humility and grace towards others.

Lord Jesus, how grateful we are that you came not to show judgment to sinners, but to offer forgiveness to us; not to point out all our sins, but to show the way and the truth and the life. How grateful we are that you continue to save us from our sins, that you forgive us and show us mercy, and that you have called us who have received mercy to give mercy. Help us to be the kind of followers who welcome people and love them in your name. Help us to live that life of love not just in church but in our lives every day. In your holy name. Amen.

Epilogue:
Beyond Platitudes, Clichés, and Half Truths

Most of us at times have believed and repeated at least some of the half truths we've considered in this book. I suspect that early in my Christian life I believed all of them. The longer and more deeply we hold these beliefs, the more unnerving or threatening it is to have them questioned.

I received a Christmas card from a man of deep faith, a biblical scholar whose view of Scripture changed as a result of some of the ideas I've shared in Chapter 4. He noted, "The changes were painful for me, but I'm grateful you were willing to stick your neck out."

What led me to question these ideas for myself? It was in part learning more about the Bible, thanks to my college and seminary professors who helped me question some of my theological assumptions. It was years of reading and studying the Bible and preaching and teaching it week after week. But largely I began to question these half truths as the result of pastoral ministry with people I cared about.

That pastoral concern is the reason I wrote this book. Were it not that these half truths have a tendency to inflict harm on people or turn them away from faith, we might simply "think and let think." Even so, I will seldom challenge someone who utters one of these statements, unless I sense that either they themselves are struggling with the statement or that their words are in danger of hurting someone else.

I spoke to a man recently who had lost his wife to cancer. He shared his grief and then said, "Pastor, I just don't understand why God had to take my wife." As we talked, I gently shared with him that I did not believe God gives people cancer and that his wife's death was the result of an illness, not the will of God. He felt liberated by the idea that God had not willed his wife's death, that God had grieved with him, and that God had not taken his wife but had embraced her at her death.

A woman came to see me after her daughter had told the family she was gay. That news was devastating to the woman on multiple levels. She told me she had been raised in a conservative Christian home, and her view of Scripture was very much like "God said it, I believe it, that settles it." Likewise she herself had frequently said of gay people, "Love the sinner, hate the sin."

This woman had "tolerated" what she had seen as my liberal understanding of Scripture regarding homosexuality, but now that the question was about her own daughter, she found herself deeply conflicted and confused. My conversation with her resembled the conversation I've had with you in Chapters 4 and 5 of this book. Just this past week I saw that mother in worship with her daughter. I believe the ideas that she and I discussed have played a role in the relationship they now have and in both mother and daughter's continued faith in Christ.

I'd like to end this book by reminding you of the "whole truths" we found behind the half truths we have rejected.

We reject the idea that everything that happens is God's will. Instead we say that whatever happens,

God is able to able to work through it, to redeem it, and to bring good from it.

We reject the idea that God only helps those who help themselves. We recognize that God expects us to do what we can to help ourselves. We pray and we work. But ultimately the very definition of grace and mercy is that God helps those who cannot help themselves.

We reject the idea that God won't give us more than we can handle. This is partly because we reject the idea that whatever adversity we face is given to us by God. What we do believe is that God will help us handle all the adversity life will give us.

We reject the idea that every verse of Scripture should be read, out of context, as the literal words of God. Instead we recognize that the biblical authors were people, influenced by God but not merely stenographers. Like all of us they were shaped by, and responded to, the historical circumstances in which they lived. And thus we believe that, when they are rightly interpreted, God speaks through the words of Scripture in order to teach, guide, shape, and encourage us.

Finally, we reject the notion that God calls upon Christians to "love the sinner, hate the sin." When we choose to focus on the sins of others and speak of hating *their* sin, we violate the words and spirit of Jesus. Paul calls us to hate *our* sins, and Jesus calls us to love our *neighbors*, all of whom are sinners. When we demonstrate love and not judgment, we draw people to Christ rather than repel them from him.

Half truths confuse, discourage, and often alienate people from God. The whole truths we've discussed give hope and encouragement and draw people to God. Let's set aside the half truths, eliminating them from our theological vocabulary, and, in their place, let's share and live the whole truths that God doesn't cause evil but redeems it. Let's share that God helps those who cannot help themselves. Let's seek to be the people through whom God works to help people handle all that life gives them. Let's read Scripture not as divine dictation, but as the witness and reflections of God's people, influenced by the Spirit yet leaving room for questions. And let's be people whose lives and faith are defined by our willingness to love.

Notes

1. John Calvin, *Institutes of the Christian Religion*, trans. Henry Beveridge (Grand Rapids: Wm. B. Eerdmans, 1989), 178.

2. Ibid., 180.

3. Adapted from my book, *Seeing Gray in a World of Black and White* (Nashville: Abingdon Press, 2008).

4. John Patrick Daly, *When Slavery Was Called Freedom* (Lexington: University Press of Kentucky, 2002), 31.

5. Sandra Chambers, "Billy Graham: A Faithful Witness," *CharismaNews*, November 7, 2013. http://www.charismanews.com/us/41684-billy-graham-a-faithful-witness?showall=1. Originally published in *Charisma* (2005).

ACKNOWLEDGMENTS

The chapters in this book began as sermons I preached at the United Methodist Church of the Resurrection. I wake up each day grateful to serve as their senior pastor. So much of this book was shaped by my ministry with the people of this congregation.

I'm also grateful for my wife, LaVon, who patiently tolerated the many times I was writing late nights, on my day off, and while we were on vacation in order to prepare this book. She is a saint.

Special thanks to my terrific team at Abingdon Press. Susan Salley serves as a partner and fellow dreamer in developing this and most of my books. Ron Kidd is my editorial partner in making sure the ideas I hope to communicate actually make sense. I'm grateful to Randy Horick who took my sermon manuscripts and from them created the first draft of this book. Thanks, Randy!

In addition, I'm indebted to the rest of the team at Abingdon who work to design, market, and in a thousand other ways allow my books to see the light of day. They are too numerous to mention, but those I work most closely with include Alan Vermilye, Tamara Crabtree, and Brenda Smotherman, as well as Mary Bernard at the A Group.

The team at United Methodist Communications did a great job of designing, filming, editing, and producing the videos on the DVD that goes with this book. Thanks, too, to Thistle Farms for hosting me, the film crew, and our studio audience. The audience was made up of seminary students, pastors, and staff members of Nashville churches; it was a joy to spend time with them.

Finally, I'd like to thank the churches that have used my books for small group studies, Sunday school classes, youth groups, and as the basis for sermon series. As I began writing this book, and throughout the development process, I prayed that God might use it to encourage, bless, challenge, and strengthen the faith of readers, and that it might also help nonreligious and nominally religious people to rediscover God's grace and love.

Adam Hamilton
April 2016

About the Author

ADAM HAMILTON is senior pastor of The United Methodist Church of the Resurrection in the Kansas City area with an average weekly attendance of over 10,000. It has been cited as the most influential mainline church in America. Hamilton speaks across the U.S. each year on leadership and connecting with nonreligious and nominally religious people. In 2013 the White House invited him to preach at the National Prayer Service as part of the presidential inauguration festivities. In 2016 he was appointed to the President's Advisory Council on Faith-Based and Neighborhood Partnerships.

A master at explaining questions of faith in a down-to-earth fashion, he is the author of many books including *The Journey*, *The Way*, *24 Hours That Changed the World*, *Enough*, *Why: Making Sense of God's Will*, *When Christians Get it Wrong*, *Seeing Gray in a World of Black and White*, *Forgiveness*, *Love to Stay*, and *Making Sense of the Bible*. To learn more about Adam and to follow his regular blog postings, visit www.AdamHamilton.com.

WATCH VIDEOS BASED ON *HALF TRUTHS* WITH ADAM HAMILTON THROUGH AMPLIFY MEDIA.

Amplify Media is a multimedia platform that delivers high quality, searchable content with an emphasis on Wesleyan perspectives for churchwide, group, or individual use on any device at any time. In a world of sometimes overwhelming choices, Amplify gives church leaders and congregants media capabilities that are contemporary, relevant, effective and, most importantly, affordable and sustainable.

With *Amplify Media* church leaders can:

- Provide a reliable source of Christian content through a Wesleyan lens for teaching, training, and inspiration in a customizable library
- Deliver their own preaching and worship content in a way the congregation knows and appreciates
- Build the church's capacity to innovate with engaging content and accessible technology
- Equip the congregation to better understand the Bible and its application
- Deepen discipleship beyond the church walls

Ask your group leader or pastor about Amplify Media and sign up today at www.AmplifyMedia.com.